D0356570

How Your Child Is Smart

A Life-Changing Approach to Learning

Dawna Markova, Ph.D.
with Anne Powell

Foreword by Peter M. Senge

Conari Press
Berkeley, CA

*To the children,
our true abundance.*

Copyright © 1992 by Dawna Markova and Anne Powell.
Foreword © 1992 by Peter M. Senge.

All Rights Reserved. No part of this book may be used or reproduced in any manner whatsoever without written permission, except in the case of brief quotations in critical articles or reviews. For information, contact Conari Press, 2550 Ninth Street, Suite 101, Berkeley, CA 94710.

Printed and bound in Australia by Cranbrook Colour for Switched On Publications, Phone: (07) 341 4490.

Cover: Fassino Design

Printed in the United States of America on recycled paper.
ISBN: 0-943233-38-0

Library of **Congress Cataloging-in-Publication Data**

Markova, Dawna, 1942–
    How your child is smart : a life-changing approach to learning / by Dawna Markova with Anne Powell.
        p.   cm.
    Includes index.
    ISBN 0-943233-38-0
1. Learning, Psychology of.   2. Thought and thinking—Study and teaching (Elementary)—United States. Education, Elementary—United States—Parent Participation.   I. Powell, Anne, 1950– II. Title.
LB1060.M335   1992
370.15'23—dc20   92-489

Contents

Our deep and heartfelt appreciation to those whose fingerprints cover every page of this book

With limitless love:
David Peck
Bruce and Brian Veivia
Edith and William Mechanic
Joan, Lewis, Thomas, and James Sapiro
Annie Phillips
Peggy and Paul Powell
Phil, Curt, and Steve Powell

With practical inspiration:
Milton Erickson, M.D., Edward Hall, Richard Kuboyama
Lloyd Miyashiro, Peter Senge
The children who have been our teachers

With steady alliance:
Catherine Devine, Brad Hunsaker
Ruth Anderson, Lucy Lorin, Reece Michaelson, Suzanne Weinberg
Susan Koen, Bea Mah Holland, Jody Whelden
Jean Boughton, Joan Caplan, Ed Mead
Marybeth Home, Tracey Nardone, Carol O'Connor
Rita Luk, Martha Batten, Mary DeCant, Linda Artz,
Sally Robertson McGrath
The East Coast Advanced Study Group
The students and faculty of Brimfield Elementary School
The teachers and administrators of Dracut Public Schools

With unbounded hearts and unbendable arms:
Andy Bryner
Peris Gumz

And to those who made it happen with magic, muscle, and unrelenting belief:
Julie Bennett, Karen Bouris, Will Glennon
Dale La Pointe, Diane Fassino

*We embrace, with particular gratitude, Mary Jane Ryan,
who has ears in her heart that heard our souls whisper
and turned it all to ink.*

Foreword

Anyone who is paying attention today knows that America is in trouble. The conditions in our cities speak deeply of fragmentation, dislocation, disenfranchisement, hopelessness, anger. These are deep problems. We know this in our hearts but we are unsure what, if anything, can be done.

I spend most of my time working within the business community, where the quest is for improved international competitiveness, "total quality," productivity, empowerment. Many of us, both theorists and practitioners, are coming to believe that the real challenge goes beyond the buzzwords—it is to learn how to learn, together. The real quest is for "learning organizations," organizations that continually generate knowledge—for knowledge, innovativeness, and the capacity for creativity are the only reliable sources of competitive advantage in a world of accelerating change and increasing interdependence.

There's only one problem. Most of us have forgotten what we once knew; we have forgotten what it means to live life as a learner. And it is no coincidence. Herein lies the connection between the breakdown of our communities and our stumbling efforts for global competitiveness.

"Our prevailing system of management has destroyed our people," states the venerable pioneer of quality management, Dr. W. Edwards Deming. "People are born with intrinsic motivation, self-esteem, dignity, curiosity to learn, joy in learning. The destruction begins with toddlers—a prize for the best Halloween costume, grades in school, gold stars—and on up through the university. On the job people, teams, divisions are ranked--reward for the one at the top, punishment for the one at the bottom."

The "system of management" Deming points to is not something taught only in business schools or Fortune 500 companies. It is a deep set of culturally-embedded beliefs and practices that manifest in social institutions profoundly inconsistent with human nature. Human beings are designed to learn. "The drive to learn," says the anthropologist Edward T. Hall, "is more basic than the drive to reproduce." Our primary social institutions, work and school, are designed to control—and with the breakdown of our family structures, these institutions are increasingly pivotal in shaping social norms and behaviors.

The young child learns very quickly that school is not about learning. School is about avoiding mistakes. School is about getting the right answers. School is about gaining approval and avoiding disapproval. These are the same lessons the first time worker learns. Don't screw up, do what you're told, if something is screwed up make sure you don't get blamed, at all costs look good.

This profound mismatch between our intrinsic drive to learn and our institutions' drive to control thwarts the continual unfolding of our natural curiosity, capacity for invention, love of experimentation, sense of wonder, sense of connection. At some level, the scars are equally severe for those who "succeed" in the "education" system as for those who fail. The "winners" have so much vested in what they know and in "being right" that they become, as Harvard's Chris Argyris puts it, "smart people who cannot learn." They populate the highest ranks of our organizations and reinforce the predominant norms of looking good, being right, and staying in control. The "losers," and evidence suggests that in their own minds these are really the vast majority of young people, simply become lifelong failures, labeled by society and themselves as not able.

Yes, the smoke may have been rising over South Central Los Angeles, but the fire is smoldering in Chicago, New York, and Atlanta—no less so in the suburbs of Miami, Dallas, and Phoenix. We are failing our children. And, no society can do that for long without paying the price.

Many confronting the deeper nature of our problems cry out that the solution lies in "fixing education." But you cannot "fix" a structure that was never designed for learning in the first place.

Moreover, the "fix education" movement identifies the problem as somewhere "out there," something caused by incompetent teachers, or non-innovative bureaucrats, or lack of funds. It absolves us of responsibility for the real task—rebuilding the system whereby our children are educated from the foundation up. This will involve questioning basic assumptions, like some kids are smart and some are not. It will involve engaging in a reciprocal process of reflection and inquiry, understanding the unique ways in which each of us learns, adult and child. It will require confronting the pain each of us has experienced in school and work when we discovered that nobody really cared about our ideas, our questions, our dreams. This is not a job that can be delegated. We will all have to re-enter the sacred space of *being* a learner.

Dawna Markova started off to write this book for teachers and educators. But she and co-author Anne Powell eventually discovered that "the impetus" for the types of change needed today must come from parents, "the first and foremost guardians of our children's minds."

So, this book is written for us as parents. And for us as members of a community in stress. It is an invitation to re-engage in perhaps the oldest of social responsibilities, nurturing our young. Perhaps, as we do this, we will rediscover the meaning of an old African proverb, that "It takes an entire village to raise a child."

Perhaps we will also begin to rediscover the original meaning of "educate," the Latin *educare*, to lead out. For, if there is anything needed in our society today, it's the capacity to lead ourselves out.

Peter M. Senge
Center for Organizational Learning, MIT

It's Not How Smart Your Child Is, It's How Your Child Is Smart

"We do not inherit the world from our parents, we borrow it from our children."

—Mahatma Gandhi

We write this book as parents. We write this book for parents and others who guide children: stepparents, friends, teachers, relatives, counselors. We write this book because too many of us have been holding ourselves back for too long in the wrong places. We believe it is time for individual parents to break their silence and talk to each other and the people in schools about what we *do* know about the abilities and needs of our children. We believe it is time to join together and be led, not by standardized tests and experts who have never met our children, but by what we and our children know to be true.

We have written this book to profoundly change the way you and schools have been taught to think about your children's abilities. We have written it to quietly empower you and them. We do not wish to change you. We do not wish to change your children. Instead, we wish to change the way you both think about what they are and are not capable of doing, learning, and knowing.

Initially, we thought this book would be addressed to educators. We understand teachers. We are teachers. We understand what it is to contain the pressure of so much responsibility with so little support: increased class size, diminished services, supplies, safety. But we've come to realize that the impetus for change must come from parents, the first and foremost guardians of our children's minds.

It is not our intention to foster a revolution against schools or teachers. Indeed, we believe this approach to comprehending

1

how children think, learn, and communicate can be profoundly supportive to the real purpose of quality education. Thus, this book is not exclusively for parents, but we believe it is parents who will lead the way to the creation of a grassroots evolution within the schools.

We understand parents. We are parents. We understand both your undivided commitment to your children and your frustration. It *is* possible to make a difference. Everything that exists in the world of human effort was created by someone who refused to accept the unacceptable. In the pages that follow, we would like to help you find strength to rely on the authority of your own experience and remain true to your own deep purpose in parenting. We wish to encourage you to take responsibility for supporting an educational system that honors the fullness of diversity in learning.

The material in this book is based on years of experience, both in and out of the classroom. It is grounded in clinical and educational psychology, perceptual modalities, learning theory, hypnotherapy, and expressive art therapy, but it is not a theoretical work. It is designed to be immediately accessible and helpful to every parent, regardless of educational background.

This book is intended not to lead you, but to serve as a companion while you guide your own curiosity to your children's talents, accomplishments, and educational needs. There are qualities and abilities in them which are as yet unrecognized. They are living far below their full capacity. We offer this book as an ally to help you and everyone involved with your children discover their unique capabilities and realize just how they *are* smart.

From Dawna:

I have been learning about learning for almost fifty years: as a student, a teacher, a parent, a psychotherapist, and an educational consultant. In the past three decades, I have taught kindergarten through the doctoral level, in public schools from the inner city of New York to migrant labor camps, from rural New Hampshire to suburban New York. I have served as classroom teacher, learning specialist, teacher trainer, Title One Coordinator, and educational psychologist. My special delight has been working with the kids no one else wanted to teach, the "hopeless cases" that had more labels than Campbell's Soup. Rather than giving up on them, I have attempted to give to them the gift of themselves by teaching them how to use and trust their own minds.

Since writing *The Art of the Possible: A Compassionate Approach to Understanding the Way People Think, Learn, and Communicate,* I have been besieged by impassioned parents who want to know how to understand their children and get their children to understand them. They feel education is failing, and complain that even those children who seem to be "succeeding" in school are using only a small portion of their abilities, rapidly losing self-esteem, and becoming resigned and cynical.

I care deeply about children. And I don't like what we are doing to them in our schools. I don't like it at all. I refuse to shrug. I refuse to wait any longer for things to get better, for someone else to do something. I refuse to accept the unacceptable.

I am committed to helping people of all ages learn to access and use the inner resources they already have to the fullest. I want to help parents help their children learn to use their minds fully, joyously, and creatively instead of having them abused, misused, or refused.

From Anne:

My deep love and respect for children and my passionate belief that learning can be an empowering, lifelong process have brought me to the writing of this book. I come to it as a student who had the most profound learning experience of my life when taught by Dawna about how my mind works. I come to it as a parent who has supported my son's growth and aliveness for six

3

years and who is determined to see that his curiosity is deepened, not dampened, by his schooling. I come to it as a teacher of ten years, who experienced many magical moments in the classroom when I intuitively made a positive difference in some child's sense of who she was and what he could do. I come as a teacher of teachers, intent on passing on some simple clues that can help those moments happen more often. I come as one who knows the frustration of trying to make long-lasting changes in an overburdened educational system in all of these roles.

For the last five years, with Dawna's support and guidance, I have taught several hundred individuals about personal thinking patterns. Funded by a grant from the Commonwealth Inservice Institute, I worked with classroom teachers, special education teachers, and the school psychologist at the Brimfield Elementary School in Massachusetts during the 1989-90 school year. The teachers began to identify their students' thinking patterns and learned how to plan lessons that would more completely meet the various needs of the children in their care. In Dracut, Massachusetts, I taught this approach to elementary and secondary teachers as part of a substance abuse prevention course given through a local college. In only three sessions, we were able to provide teachers with insight and suggestions as to how to adapt their teaching styles and increase their effectiveness with these troubled students.

In working with individuals, parents and their children, teachers and administrators, I have experienced the pervasive, natural human desire to understand ourselves and each other. The assumption that parents and teachers are somehow adversaries is inaccurate, dehumanizing, and disempowering to us all. My experience shows me that this common sense, easy-to-grasp information can help us find the path that leads us back to our compassion and support for each other, and can become a bridge that brings us together in our common goal to support the unfurling of our children's minds.

4

It is my hope that in reading this book, you can learn about how your child learns, retrieve much of what you already know about your child's mind, validate it in a new light, and find the support, courage, and skills to share what you know with your child's teachers. It is my hope that teachers, in turn, can use this information to learn how to enjoy your child more in their classrooms and help maximize his or her potential.

From Both of Us:

There's no question that education in this country is deep in the midst of a crisis. There's no shortage of solutions offered by experts. At the bottom of it all, though, we believe our schools are failing because they don't know how to facilitate learning. Learning is not only acquiring new information—in fact that's only a small part of it. Learning is also helping children expand their ability to be effective in their lives. It means teaching them to develop a relationship of trust with their own minds so they can generate new possibilities, so they can create, relate, and make a difference.

To turn things around, parents and teachers need to shift from being the "learning experts" to becoming facilitators of learning. We all need to be focused on learning how our children learn rather than concentrating on controlling their minds to acquire information that will be outdated before it can even be integrated. And that means beginning to recognize, honor, and respect the different ways children learn.

At a time when schools are failing and students are being seriously shortchanged, you can no longer shrug or wait for someone who will come along and care enough to protect and empower your children's minds. It's more crucial than ever that parents play a key role in guiding their children's education. We write this book so you will be able to be the "someone who" can make that difference for your child.

1

The Differences that Make a Difference

"We suppress our children and then when they lack a natural interest in learning, they are offered special coaching for their scholastic difficulties."
—Alice Miller

You need a certain amount of nerve to be a parent, an almost physical nerve. You need to know when to hold on tightly, and when to hold yourself back and let go. You need to know when to give encouragement, when to give information, and when to give room for mistakes to be made. You need to know your child can fall and survive. Above all, you need to know how to transfer your child's trust from your strength and center of balance to his or her own.

Many years ago, I heard a poignant story from Elizabeth Kubler-Ross, a powerful woman who has worked extensively with the terminally ill. She told of two parents whose youngest son was dying of cancer. What he wanted more than anything else before he died was to ride his two-wheeled bicycle alone around the block without training wheels. She described how the parents stood at the top of the driveway, holding their breath, arms wrapped tightly around their chests. As their frail and vulnerable child kept falling down, climbing up on the bike, pedaling a few feet, and falling down again, they knew they had to hold themselves back.

While listening to Elizabeth tell the story, I dug my nails into my sides. Every cell in my body was standing at the top of that driveway with those two parents I had never met. David, my own son, is strong and healthy. I write this book as he celebrates his twenty-fifth birthday. A few months ago, I stood at the top of our driveway watching him drive off on a journey across the country to make his own home. He left a vapor trail of memories behind: I thought of the times I wasn't sure if either of us would make it, the times I had to hold myself back and let him fall, the times I had to stand up for him as his only advocate, the one who knew his strengths and limitations and was willing to fight for him. The times I wasn't. Or couldn't.

For the most part, we all stumble through the challenges we have to face with our children unsupported and unprepared. There are so few guidelines to follow, because the world changes as fast as our children do, and the old ways just don't work anymore. Skateboards are very different from two-wheelers, and roller blades stranger still. How do we support, guide, and encourage our children so they will be able to handle themselves in the stiffest of winds? How do we shift their trust and belief in us to themselves, so they have an indwelling center of power and self-esteem that they can count on over the steepest of hills?

These questions nag at you from the moment your children are born. Their pressure increases as your children begin to attend school. Will they be challenged? Can they learn the skills they will need in their lives? Will they be as good, as bright, as talented as other children? Will the teacher be kind to them? Will they be safe? Should you intervene? How much? Should you push them, coerce them, mold and cajole them into doing what is required of them? Will your children have to sacrifice their uniqueness in order to learn? Will they be labeled, disabled, unable to make it on their own? Will the school recognize how your children are smart? Should you tell them?

What makes the task even more frustrating is that each child seems to need a different kind of parenting for the very same task. In learning to ride a bike, my nephew Jimmy wanted to be shown every detail—where to put his feet, how to push the pedals, how to turn the handlebars. Then he wanted to be left in the quiet to carefully make his way down the road. His older brother Tommy, however, insisted that his father just let him figure it out. He didn't watch, wouldn't listen to any instructions. Rather he was immediately off on his own bloody adventure, willing to fall until he got it right, expecting applause and encouragement when he returned.

Instinctively we notice these differences in how children learn, but as we send them off to school, we fail to realize that these very differences make a difference in whether our children succeed or not.

◆ ◆ ◆

One day when I was working as a learning specialist, I sat in the principal's office sipping coffee from a styrofoam cup. A freshman had been having difficulty in English and social studies. He'd been referred to the school psychologist for testing, which took three hours. Four weeks later, the results had been evaluated, and all of us who were responsible for his education that year—classroom teachers, guidance counselor, assistant principal, and me—were being enlightened.

The psychologist's metal-rimmed glasses kept slipping down his thin nose as he summarized his findings by describing the percentile ratings, medians, means, and norms of the boy's disabilities. His eyes never left the charts and papers as he gave a detailed profile of the student's deficits, and by the end of an hour, we all knew everything this young man could not do as well as the average or normal ninth grader. I could not keep from yawning, in spite of the caffeine and maple-glazed doughnuts.

Finally, I piped up. "Excuse me, Mr. Baron, but could you please tell us what this boy's *strengths* are, what he *can* do well?"

You didn't have to be a psychologist to know Mr. Baron was not pleased with my question. He cleared his throat, adjusted his gold cuff links, and explained that this student had many problems, as well as a home situation that was less than ideal.

"Yes," I replied, "But if you don't mind my saying so, if we knew some of his strengths, his assets, we might be able to figure out how to use them to overcome those challenges."

Mr. Baron scowled over the tops of his glasses and said curtly that we would discuss the matter at our next staff meeting in a month. The discussion never occurred.

As a result of that incident and many others like it, at the end of that school year, I felt ironed flat, gray as cardboard. I left public education.

When I returned five years later, it was only because I needed a temporary job. But what I discovered helped me begin to understand that mental capability is like a water table beneath the surface of the earth. No one owns it and anyone can be taught to tap into it.

I didn't want to go back to teaching. I was hunched over believing what the doctors had told me—that I was terminally ill. I really just wanted a job that would pay the rent and keep David in Devil Dogs and Fruit Loops. I went to the local middle school and asked for a job as a substitute teacher. The assistant principal had a carefully trimmed mustache, and was as stiff as cellophane. His name was a compass direction, something like Mr. West. He told me he would phone if there was an opening. Just as I turned to leave, he cleared his throat and called me back. He was looking at my resume, and mumbling something about my experience with "problem" students. I explained I was only available for temporary work. Mr. West began to talk about an experimental class of seventh, eighth, and ninth grade students.

"To be honest," he said, "what we did was take all the kids that the teachers refused to have in their classes and lump them together. The man who was their teacher had a breakdown. I've tried six different substitutes in the four weeks since he left. I was hoping for a large male type, but you do have this experience in Harlem and migrant labor camps. You don't look very strong, though. Do you know karate by any chance?"

I didn't know karate, but I did know what was going on. The school was 95 percent upper middle class children whose parents were professors at the nearby Ivy League college. The kids in *this* particular class were from local farms and the railroad town that was home for the gardeners, gas station attendants, and employees of the local Winn Dixie.

I surprised myself by agreeing to the job immediately. I figured that it would keep my mind off the pain that had taken over my body. Besides, what did I have to lose? My career had three months until termination, or so medical science had said. More important things than a bunch of testosterone-tortured teenagers were intimidating me.

There were at least eight boom-boxes playing different music simultaneously at full blast as I walked in the classroom. A few girls were either dancing or having some kind of seizure on top of the desks. Some couples were necking, making out, going at it under the desks. Everyone else was seething in the corners. All together they reminded me of some kind of great beast plagued by fleas.

There were no windows in the classroom. I shut off the fluorescent lights. I never could stand them. I had just read an article by a man in Florida who said they made kids hyperactive. These kids did not need to be made any more hyperactive.

When the lights went out, everything got dark. I did the only thing I could think of to do. I sat down on the floor. For a while the wild beast pretended not to notice I was there. It took four full minutes for them to acknowledge my presence. Someone shouted, "Hey, lady, what are you doing on the floor?" I just breathed. I couldn't think of a single reply. More minutes went by. Two girls went around the room turning off the boom-boxes. No one turned the lights back on. I don't know why. The great beast turned towards me and opened its jaws. "We asked you *why* you're sitting on the floor, lady. You better answer us, bitch, we've put away six teachers already."

The words fell out of my mouth. "I need the money."

That's all I said. My voice echoed off the wall. Then, most of the beast slid down to the floor and sat around me, curious.

I did what I always do when I am scared, I started talking, fast. "I used to love to teach. I loved turning kids on to their own minds. But I'd be lying if I told you that's why I'm here." I had their attention. Teachers never admitted to lying.

"I'm terrified right now. I'll probably fail just as bad, maybe worse, as those other substitute teachers. But I need the money."

It was the truth. They knew it. They didn't have any smart comebacks. They just shut up and listened.

"You kids got stuck in here because they thought you were failures. Well, this is where *I* belong then, because I'm more of a failure than you'll ever be. I'm going to be dead in three months. That's the truth. I'm here to make some money so my kid and I can eat until then."

I paused and took some deep breaths. Some of the kids seemed to breathe with me. "You probably won't know any more when I leave than you do right now and I'll be to blame. I'm sorry you lucked out and got me as a teacher. But we're in the same place, 'cause you're just putting in time until you can leave and I'm putting in time until I *have* to leave."

No one said a thing for many minutes. There were some

shuffling feet, some throats cleared. They had no idea how to deal with me. Teachers were *not* supposed to tell the truth. Teachers were *not* supposed to admit they could fail. Teachers were *not* supposed to take the blame or apologize to the kids or to sit on the floor in the dark and say they're going to die.

I took a yellow plastic mini-flashlight out of my leather pocketbook. (Everything in those days was micro or mini.) I pulled out a book and began to read to myself, ignoring the beast as it rumbled around me. One student, Denise, who had blond hair ironed straight, and black stockinged legs stretching from a denim mini-micro skirt, asked me what I was reading. I told her it was *The Diary of Anne Frank* and was about a teenage girl who was trapped in an attic during World War II. I explained how she had to live in the dark each night so the Nazis wouldn't find her family. I began to read aloud.

Sixty-five minutes later, I looked up and noticed the beast had rolled over, belly-up, ready to be scratched. Everyone in the room had a slack jaw and half-closed eyes. We had all been in that dark attic with Anne. Together. In the weeks that followed, I was told by the psychologist that these kids' maximum attention span was ten minutes. Obviously, their maximum attention span was ten minutes when they were *bored*. Everyone was always talking about these kids' inabilities, but what they were really talking about was their own inability to interest these kids.

So rather than concentrating on what they couldn't do, I began to spend a lot of time sitting on the edge of a metal desk just being plain old curious, forgetting what I had been told about what was wrong with these kids. They may have been lost in a world of paper, but there were worlds in which their various intelligences could be found. The standardized IQ tests told me how unsmart they were, but when I was willing to get dumb enough to notice, it became obvious how these discarded, disabled, dyslexic kids *were* smart.

I began to make my mind work the way theirs did. I spent my evenings with my eyes shut and my body wiggling the way Joe's did. I'd hear people talking to me and immediately forget what they had said the way Samantha did. Instead of bringing cumulative folders home in my briefcase each night, I carried a different child in my heart.

Since these kids did not come equipped with an instructional manual, and since it was obvious there was no one right way to teach them, I began to experiment. Joe was thirteen and classified as dyslexic, which simply meant he couldn't read. After spending an evening "Joethinking," I realized that he was very aware of his body, and had a highly developed sense of touch. A few days later, he was in an accident with a blasting cap which left him blind. The loss of his sight actually facilitated his learning to read. I asked a blind high school student to teach both Joe and me to read Braille. His fingers learned in a way mine never could. In a few months, he was reading prolifically for the first time in his life. He was even giving remedial Braille lessons to his "dyslexic" learning specialist!

I asked why so many of these kids were being given Ritalin. The school psychologist patiently explained that Ritalin had a paradoxical effect on hyperactive children. While it speeded up adults in a similar fashion to caffeine, it slowed down children that were speedy and supposedly allowed them to focus and attend for longer periods of time. I said that I had read some research that indicated it might have harmful side effects on developing bodies and in some cases was being used inappropriately for kids who really just needed to learn by doing and moving. I suggested that in addition to or instead of medication, we could find other ways to help children attend to task and communicate.

I was repeatedly told these students were resistant, but

when I worked with them on things that interested them, when I taught them to identify how their minds work and what they needed, when I coached them in evaluating their own progress, there was no resistance to be found. Their test scores climbed upward. Slowly at first, and then steadily and more rapidly.

The school board members began to complain that my methodology was unconventional, and therefore faulty in some way. Different was, of course, wrong. The assistant principal came into the classroom to observe. One group of kids was dressed up as "The Mamas and The Papas," a famous rock group, and were singing their spelling words onto a tape recorder. Another bunch was setting up a printing press, which was going to be used to publish the class's newspaper (in an original, secret language). A young man in the corner was pounding on a punching bag which was held by two other kids. Two girls were curled under my desk reading to a third. A boy wearing a cardboard sign around his neck that said 'Leave me alone, I'm having a Goof Day' was elbow deep in sculpting clay. When the bell rang at three o'clock, no one rushed for the door; no one even moved, as a matter of fact. That's not quite true. Mr. West rushed out to the school buses, scratching his head in confusion.

None of us in that classroom failed. I did not die. Shirley learned how to read, Peanuts how to spell, Danny how to multiply. I did not have to add anything to their minds to "get them" to learn. Mostly, I was involved in subtracting some of the obstacles that had been placed between those kids and their own internal resources. Perhaps I was their un-teacher.

Ultimately though, I did fail. The light that was in their eyes when they entered school was never rekindled. Their cumulative folders and their minds had been so filled with descriptions of their deficits, disabilities, and dilemmas that they ultimately became self-fulfilling prophecies. Danny dropped out of school two years later, joined the Marines, and was killed in Vietnam. Peanuts ended up in prison at seventeen, and Shirley got pregnant at fifteen and probably still works at the cash register of the local Winn Dixie.

◆ ◆ ◆

After all these years of working with children in public schools, and adults in private practice and training workshops, it is obvious to me that a significant portion of what we have come to think of as psychological problems or learning disabilities are actually caused by misunderstandings of how children's minds work. We just don't all think and learn the same way and in order to properly educate our children, we must come to understand the nature of the different ways they use their minds.

There was one child I would like to tell you about who had a major impact on my understanding of how to help children learn. He has been the inspiration for my understanding of the differences that make a difference in learning. His name was Jerome, and he was a fourteen-year-old sixth grader living in a migrant labor camp with his aunt and two sisters in a small Florida town. I was the school psychologist. My office was a former broom closet. Jerome was referred to me because he could not read, and because no one else knew what to do with him.

His cumulative folder said that he had been classified as trainable retarded, which meant don't bother trying to teach him to read. He was a big kid, even for fourteen, and had both mischief and misery in his brown eyes. He told me the first day not to bother trying to teach him because he wasn't going to ever learn. That made it unanimous. And a challenge. I do love challenges.

I learned from some of the other kids that Jerome was the

chess champion of the camp. You and I know you can't play chess well if you're stupid. I went to watch him play one night, which was evidently rather unusual. No white teacher had ever stepped foot in that camp. I found Jerome surrounded by a small crowd. His opponent was a man in his mid-forties. Everyone was sitting or squatting on boxes except for our hero who was pacing, back and forth. No one made a sound. His eyes scanned the board, he paced and then quickly made his move, declaring "checkmate."

I was fascinated. I spent days trying to make my mind work like his. Finally, I brought a large book into my office with the title, *A Black History of America,* spelled out in gold letters across the cover. Jerome had never seen a book with photographs of African-Americans. He did everything he could think of to try and get me to read it to him. Finally I offered to play a game of chess with him, but only on the following terms: if he won, I'd read it to him. If I won, he'd have to learn to read it even if it took all year.

It must have been divine intervention. I was a beginning chess player and Jerome was definitely an expert, but I won that game. And it took us the rest of the school year, but Jerome did learn to read that book. He had figured out how his mind had learned to play chess and told me about it: "I gotta be standing up and moving around. And it's gotta be real quiet or I can't think. Then I gotta look steady with my eyes at one thing, and one thing only, like the chess board, then I gotta close my eyes and see it in my mind, then I hear way inside my mind what to do."

To teach him to read, I needed to follow the same pattern. So phonics were out! Instead, while he was moving with his eyes closed, I spelled words out loud, tracing them on his back or in his palm. He'd say it while he looked at it in the book. Then he wrote it on paper. It was laborious at first, but Jerome learned very quickly. And he taught me as much as I taught him. On his last day of school, he disappeared, leaving the book behind. His sister told me he was afraid it would get stolen and that would have hurt him too much. He wrote me the following poem:

I don't know
how to show
the delight of feeling right
about what was wrong
or so they said
about my head.
Thanks.

(The statistical chances of Jerome being alive today are very slight. African-American men are an endangered species. He does live, of course, in everything I teach and touch. The essence of my approach to understanding personal thinking patterns that is the mortar of this work is a gift from Jerome. If you come to understand any of the ordinary magic of your children's extraordinary minds as a result of this book, please thank him.)

I exited public schools permanently five years after Jerome learned to read that book. It was very painful for me to leave. But when I am asked, "What's your profession? Are you a psychologist?" I still answer, "No. I'm a teacher." I left education because I could no longer survive there. It was as if I were trying to teach deep breathing in an oven with the gas turned on.

Since then, I have trained parents, counselors, social workers, teachers, psychotherapists. My decision to turn back toward American public education is because I want to share the gift I received from Jerome—the understanding that people learn in different ways. Someday, someone who reads this book will work with a sister, a cousin, a brother of Jerome's. Then the circle will be complete.

◆ ◆ ◆

The pulse of my experience with Jerome and many other children gives source to this book, for they taught me to think about how we think. They forced me to notice the differences in *how* we learn that make all the difference in *whether* we learn. Understanding those differences became the foundation for the discovery that each of us has a unique way of learning—our own process for taking information in, storing it, recalling it, and expressing it—which I call a "personal thinking pattern."

Understanding your child's pattern can be as valuable to you in helping her access her abilities as knowing how to use the automated teller machines can be for getting cash from your bank account. It can help your child know all he can know and learn all she can learn.

2

Reclaiming
Your Child's Mind

*"It is, in fact, nothing short of a miracle
that the modern methods of instruction
have not entirely strangled the holy
curiosity of inquiry."*
—Albert Einstein

Like Dorothy and her companions on their journey to find the Wizard of Oz, you send your children off to school hoping they will find their hearts, their minds, their courage, their magic, and their way back home. Too often, all too often, what they find is the Wicked Witch of the West, or a puny charlatan hiding behind a curtain pulling levers, and a failed magic.

Rather than being nurtured, encouraged, and having their natural resources developed, rather than being in a learning environment in which they can thrive, respond, and change themselves, your children become convinced that they must change the very nature of who they are. Spells are cast that shrivel their belief in their own abilities and they are taught to doubt their own minds.

This is a tragedy, for the most essential ingredient of success as a learner is self-esteem, and self-esteem is built by trusting your own mind to accomplish what is relevant in your life. In a very real sense, schooling should be about learning how to access the intelligence you have, as well as how to widen and deepen it. You should come out of school more confident in knowing how to use your mind, not less.

It's time to stop following the yellow brick road of traditional education. Your children are learning self-abuse as they travel on it instead of self-esteem; their minds are being stunted, not expanded deeper and wider with the desire to learn. It's time for us to build the old road in a new way, a way that takes your children's individual differences into account and teaches them how best to use the minds they have.

In order to do that, it's necessary to explore the yellow brick road, and how your children's minds become stunted as they follow it. It all starts with a tornado. Or so it seems when you first delve into the problem. I hate starting with the scary stuff, but we won't end there, I promise.

I'm not going to give a comprehensive analysis of the problems facing American education—the financial constraints, language barriers, adversarial relationships between teachers and administrators, the lack of national standards and family structure, the overcrowded classrooms, and the overabundance of drugs and violence in our society. You know about all of those problems and so do I. Besides, all of that is beyond your direct sphere of influence, and just makes me want to crawl into the basement and long for Aunt Em.

What I do want to do is help you become aware of what happens to your child's mind as he or she is swept up and blown through the educational process. Knowing the direction and severity of the storm will help you find what you can do immediately, now, today, with the educational system as it is, to create a shelter so that you can help reclaim your child's natural abilities. Hopefully it will also empower you to join together with other parents to become advocates for what is possible.

The first day I entered a classroom as a student I was

terrified, electrified. The first day I entered as a teacher I was terrified, electrified. The first day I entered as a parent I was terrified, electrified. What is still clear to me from all those situations is the energy of the children that was contained within those four walls. So much life and light. The air was thick with it, the pulsing aliveness, the thrumming curiosity like bees crawling on a honeycomb; there was laughter that didn't catch self-consciously in their throats, eyes that had not yet developed lids of boredom, bodies that had not yet given up their flexible dreams, faces still so hungry to know.

My many years in education have taught me that children are naturally learning-abled and we de-skill them in school. In a very real sense, they are brighter when they begin than when they leave. Brighter, as in more alert, more willing to experiment, to be wrong and laugh about it, more willing to risk and reach. Before they enter school, kids walk as if they belong on the earth, as if they are their own people, as if they trust their own minds. There is no gap between their true nature and their ability to express it.

What happens to that hum and hunger? How do those same eyes become shadowed, suspicious just a few years later? How do those bodies get rigid and closed? How do all those dreams become crushed under arms that fold tight over chests? How does a river of ashes become layered over that true nature, covering it with limiting beliefs?

The cause is our entire educational system itself. It trains children to notice what does *not* work, and thus they come to distrust their mind's very natural ability to learn. We teach them to become proficient at keeping themselves *from* learning, and articulate in all the things that are wrong with them: we evaluate that "wrongness" in blood-red ink. The teacher marks how many words they get wrong on the spelling test, not how many they get right. They are told they are "weak in math." We groove an awareness of their mistakes into their brains. Thus, they are taught to take for granted what they can do and instead concentrate on their deficits.

If I ask a group of school-aged children to name their abilities, they inevitably begin to splutter and give responses such as, "I'm pretty good at . . . um, well, I like to read the newspaper, and I know something about . . . sports, that's it, I know something about sports."

When I ask those same kids to tell me about their shortcomings, information gushes forth: "I'm very shy and just not good at speaking in front of groups. I've always been terrible in math, and I can't dance worth beans. I'm working on improving,   but . . . ."

Noticing the hole instead of the doughnut is so commonplace in our culture that we think it's natural, but it's a very ineffective way for the human brain to work. Imagine for a moment that you keep depositing money in a savings account, but when it comes time to pay your bills you forget you have any savings. You'd feel impoverished, go out and work even harder to make more money, which you'd put in the bank, forgetting that you could also use the automatic teller machine to withdraw it. You would never feel you had "enough," and always feel you were poor. Someday you might even want to take resources from someone else who seemed to have more, or perhaps you'd get so frustrated, you'd just give up altogether. That's what education may be doing to your child.

What if, instead, you were encouraged to notice what you *did* have in your account? What if you were guided to invest it in tools and projects that would bring about the results and satisfaction you truly wanted in life? What if, instead of being taught to notice what wasn't enough about you (not smart enough, not articulate enough, not creative enough), you were taught to use your strengths to overcome your weaknesses? What if you were asked *how* you learned to spell those four words you got right on the test, and then taught to use that same method on the sixteen others you still hadn't mastered?

Instead of teaching children to access their native intelligence, their natural curiosity, wonder, compassion, and responsiveness, we teach them to be afraid to admit they do not know answers. We label them in electronic categories according to their deficits. We assume that all students learn in the same way and condemn those who do not as disabled. They leave school at best bored, at worst, damaged, de-skilled, distrustful, and wounded.

We have come to label this as a normal part of growing up. As the spark grows dimmer in our children's eyes, as their shoulders hunch protectively over their chests, we shrug and remember how it was for us. But is that really how it has to be?

When Anne was a classroom teacher, on Open School Night, she gave a sheet of paper to each parent that attended. At the top she had written, "Don't ask me to teach your children as you *were* taught, but as you wanted to be taught." Has anyone ever asked *you* how you wanted to be taught or how your child does? The question was so far from what most of them experienced that the parents in her class didn't even know where to begin.

There has been much awareness and sadness recently as the world becomes conscious of the emotional and physical abuse that has been done to so many people as they are growing. The all-too-common childhood occurrences that many of us experienced "for our own good," as psychologist Alice Miller has stated, left wounds that were sutured closed with silence. As evidence of this has come to the surface, our awareness has grown of the immense suffering that has been passed from generation to generation. Change comes with this awareness, and hopefully healing.

But the wounds done to our minds are still unnoticed or

denied. And we unwittingly transmit this legacy of abuse on to our children. They learn to hate by failing—hate themselves, hate school, hate society.

Children suffer deep pain when their natural way of thinking, of absorbing and processing information, of creating and expressing is criticized, mocked, or ignored. Even if children "do well" in school, if they master the information we insist they have to know, the cost of the demise of their self-esteem, the limitation of their true capacities, is enormous. An honors high school student recently told me how she was humiliated in front of her classmates for reading a textbook instead of watching a television program. Another reported that he just assumed he'd be bored in school, "Learning is basically boring and that's all there is to it, right?" A third said that she had always dreamed of being a nurse, but in her freshman year, her guidance counselor told her she "didn't have the required smarts," so she enrolled in a secretarial program.

What are our children's true capacities? I don't think we've even really begun to know. It is estimated we only use 15 percent, at the very most, of our brains.

What are children like whose minds have not been wounded? They are strong learners who trust their own abilities: they know and can explain how they learn and recognize what they need in any given situation. They can use the resources in their environment as well as their own inner resources to satisfy those needs. They have ready access to their inventiveness, empathy, courage, intuition, concentration, and creative thought. They know how to use their bodies with joy and agility, to solve problems creatively, to participate collaboratively, to care for themselves and others, to get along, to do quality work, to improve continuously, to motivate themselves internally, and to evaluate their own performance. They know they matter, they know they are important, they know they make a difference. The Latin root word "educare" means "to lead out from within." But, in my ten years as a classroom teacher, I came to realize the truth of what Jean Houston, a prominent psychologist states: "So much of the failure in school comes directly out of boredom, which itself comes directly out of the larger failure to stimulate all those areas in the child's brain which could give him so many more ways of responding to his world."

Day after day, I noticed children being given a set of beliefs about their deficiencies, who they could and could not become, what they were capable and incapable of doing. I began to see that this very attitude was at the root of the problem. I became aware that education can limit human capacity as well as foster it.

Failing at What?

Anyone who's ever had trouble of any kind in school loves the following list of famous failures. We think of it as an aid for the dark moments, when keeping the faith in your child is most difficult. It illustrates how school success is not necessarily an indication of true ability:

Famous orator and attorney Clarence Darrow was told by his teachers and parents that he'd never be able to speak or write.

Philosopher Jean Paul Sartre had to pretend to read.

French writer Marcel Proust couldn't write a composition in school.

Agatha Christie didn't want to learn to write.

Carl Jung found mathematics classes terrifying.

Beethoven's tutor said he was hopeless as a composer. He never learned to multiply or divide.

Louisa May Alcott's teacher complained that she drew instead of doing addition.

Pablo Picasso hated school and seemed unable to learn to

read or write when other children his age were proficient.

Emile Zola scored zero in his final literature examination.

Honore de Balzac was given up on by his teachers who described him as a failure.

President Woodrow Wilson couldn't read until he was eleven.

Thomas Edison ran away from school because his teacher beat him with a cane for not paying attention and jiggling in his seat.

A Change of Heart

Experts have been trying to solve the problems of our educational system for years, decades; to make changes here, fix this over there, blame this, dump on that. We've sworn allegiance to phonics, new math, a return to the basics. But the problems of education are exactly like the problems of addiction. And making these changes is just like an alcoholic switching from vodka to wine. There has been a deterioration over a long period of time, the overall health of the system is gradually worsening, there is a growing feeling of helplessness. Temporary solutions are tried, but they leave us feeling victimized and only seem to make things worse.

A person who has been in recovery from an addiction knows that there is a big difference between making changes and having a change of heart—getting sober. What works is facing the problem—"naming it, claiming it, and re-aiming it," supporting one another in rehabilitation, revitalization, re-visioning. This is exactly what education needs.

We need to change the spirit of education as well as the skills and practices. It is not enough to solve the problem. There is no one solution. *We have to change the thinking that created the problem in the first place.*

Naming It: Some Facts

"We know, based on research, that people remember about 10% of what they hear, 20% of what they see and 90% of what they do, but we still largely use one teaching style: `I talk, you listen and you learn.'"

—Adam Urbanski,
President of American Federation of Teachers

In the United States, we throw money at schools instead of looking at how to manage the system of education; spending on education has increased more than one and one half times as fast as inflation since 1965. But money isn't necessarily the answer. Japan, for example, spends 50 percent less per child than we do and their students lead the world in advanced science and math, languages, and technical subjects. Twenty-seven percent of our students drop out; only 6 percent of Japanese students do. We spend more on buildings and administration; they spend more on teacher salaries.

Other sobering facts:

• Adequate educations are achieved by only one-half of our students.

• There are over one hundred million standardized tests administered to American school children each year.

• American business is spending billions of dollars training employees in basic reading and math skills they should have received in public schools.

• There are two million children labeled as learning disabled in this country. That is an increase of one million students in the past decade!

• Three-quarters of a million are currently taking medication for what is called "attention-deficit hyperactivity disorder." After decades of research, it has still not been demonstrated that disabling neurological dysfunctions exist in more than a minuscule number of children.

According to William Glasser in *The Quality School*, when surveyed:

• Parents said they knew there were problems, they wanted to do things differently, but they didn't know how. What they ranked as most important was learning how to understand their children and being understood by them.

• Administrators' top priorities were: improving test scores (and therefore funding), getting more students through school, and keeping discipline problems low.

• Students said what was good about school was that their friends were there. By the end of seventh grade, more than half of them thought of teachers as adversaries, felt bossed and bored. The majority of the students who were having problems believed that the teachers didn't like them, that no one cared, that their work was irrelevant and had no value.

• Teachers stated that 80 percent of students didn't complete homework satisfactorily. Most stated that they felt ineffective and pulled between students and administrators. They said that the problem was not that students were unable but they were unwilling.

The answer is not in spending more money but in re-evaluating how we spend it.

Claiming It: The Responsibility

"I began to see first grade as a violent shock to the healthy human organism. The six-year-old has just completed the most awesome learning task on this planet, mastery of spoken language, with no formal instruction whatsoever. He is in fact a master learner, happy to explore, eager to try new things. Then comes school and he gets some stunning news: he must try to learn what the teacher says when the teacher says it, whether he's ready for it or not. He must learn to stop

exploring, to reject the unfamiliar, to focus on a limited number of stimuli, to make repetitive, standard responses. He must learn—and what a hard lesson this is—that learning itself is generally dull and boring."

—George Leonard, *Walking on the Edge of the World*

When it was recently reported in a Portland, Oregon newspaper that achievement test scores were at the same low level for the third straight year, school officials commented, "It may just be that children are at their maximum learning capacity."

Andy Rooney, commenting on "Sixty Minutes," February 2, 1992, stated that there is nothing wrong with our educational system. "The reason that only 50 percent of our kids are learning is because they are dumb," he said, with all seriousness. "And they're dumb because their parents don't make them learn!"

Both comments are typical of what is commonly called "blaming the victim." Because we don't know how to fix the problem, we blame those who suffer the most from it.

In actuality, the human mind is a natural learning machine and children are not dumb. The human species has been evolving for three billion years. The drive to learn is as strong as the sex drive, except it begins earlier and lasts longer. *No* child is unmotivated.

It is not our children who are at their maximum capacity, it is our schools. Our schools and methods of instruction were designed for an agricultural society. But this is an information age, and information is changing so rapidly that what is current today will be outmoded months from now. Education needs to evolve so that rather than being taught according to the latest fad, children will learn how to use their minds to process new information. If this were the automobile industry, what we are currently doing would be the equivalent of training mechanics how to work on the steam engine when they will be faced with a garage of Maseratis!

Our children's educational needs are continuously changing, but our methods of meeting those needs have not been. We are basically doing what we've always done and getting what we've always gotten. What we need to be doing is instructing children in how they process information as well as in the information itself. We need to begin to appreciate the differences of children's minds as treasures of infinite richness waiting to be explored.

But how can children continue to be curious about their own capacities if we are only interested in their disabilities?

Warning! Labels are dangerous to a child's self-esteem and educational health. They emphasize what students cannot do. I believe we are so attached to them because school systems are given huge amounts of money for children who wear those labels. And because they relieve everyone of responsibility for having to face up to the fact that how we are teaching children does not work.

Re-Aiming It: The Possibilities

"Most of the kids in our schools today will have to be trained and retrained half a dozen times. We've got to teach them how to learn."
—Garry Caruthers, Governor of New Mexico

The greatest resource we have in this country is the skills and talents of our children. Education can no longer involve just the transfer of information, but must be devoted to bringing out those capacities children will need to survive in the twenty-first century.

I'm remembering an old tale of a prince who became a hermit as a young man. He moved into the attic of his huge, grand castle. He ate, slept, exercised, and worked there. He stayed in that one room until he was a very old man. It got quite cramped and cluttered. The rest of the castle began to deteriorate, since it was not used, but the prince was totally unaware that it even existed. Finally one day it crumbled, and the hermit was buried in its rubble.

Like the prince, we are often hermits in the castles of our own minds. We inhabit only our logical, rational attics and ignore the rest of the resources we have available to us. As parents, we know more than we allow ourselves to know about our children's minds and how they can best be served in school. We know about the basement and the kitchen. We know jiggling seems to help Johnny pay attention and that Shandra needs to sing her spelling words. We know Li Fong likes to have a list when she goes shopping but Victor does better if he's told what to buy. All we need is to learn how to use that information to assist our child.

Our children come into the world with a spark that is uniquely their own. We, their parents, are caretakers of that flame. Even if it is reduced to a tiny ember buried in a charred timber, it is our responsibility to provide the wind that will help it rekindle. Unfortunately we have been de-skilled and wounded too. We do not trust what we know about our children's abilities. We have to learn to re-perceive the damaging ways we have been taught to think about them.

Enormous problems demand whole new ways of thinking about how we have been thinking. They can challenge us to return to our ideals, to what is really important, and to respond to a changing world with flexibility, ferocity, and originality. The approach that is offered to you in this book is not *the* solution, but the evolving expression of an ideal: that the uniqueness and diversity of young people must be valued and empowered.

The Heart of an Eagle

Once upon a time, while traveling from Here to There, a woman and her young son came upon a poultry farm. The boy was very curious and pressed his face into the rusty wire fence which penned in hundreds of chickens.

"Mommy, there is a very odd chicken in this cage. He's not like the other ones at all."

As the woman peered at the bird her son was pointing to, a scraggly man in dirty clothing approached them.

"What are you doing to my chickens?" he grumbled.

"Just looking. But would you mind telling me, sir, about that odd bird who is huddled into the far corner there? It seems to me he is quite different from the other chickens. In fact, I was thinking he might be a young eagle."

"Nonsense," the farmer replied. "I've had him since he was barely a hatchling. He acts like a chicken, he eats like a chicken, therefore he *is* a chicken."

"Do you mind if we go in the cage to find out for ourselves?"

"Do what you please," he answered.

The woman and her son bent in half to fit through the makeshift door. She went down on her knees and scooped up the young bird in question.

"You are an eagle, not a chicken. You can fly. You can fly free!"

She held him above her head and tossed him in the air.

The bird flapped its wings once or twice but fell flat on its beak as it collapsed to the ground, and began to scratch in the dirt for its feed. The farmer, watching from the other side of the fence, snickered. "I told you so. The bird is a chicken, just an ordinary chicken. You're wasting your time and mine!"

As the man turned his back on them, the boy shouted, "Excuse me, mister, but would you possibly sell him to us? Since he's just an ordinary chicken, I'm sure you wouldn't miss him."

"That's fine with me. Five dollars is my price."

The woman knew it was an exorbitant amount to pay, but her son's eyes were pleading so she gave the chuckling old man the money.

The boy scooped the eagle to his chest, ran out of the cage, and down the dusty dirt road. His mother followed him to the top of a small hill.

"What are you doing here, son?"

The boy didn't answer. Instead he lifted the young bird as high as his arms would stretch and implored, "You have the heart of an eagle. I know you do. You're a fine and wonderful creature. You're meant to be free. Spread your wings, follow your heart and fly. Please eagle, fly!"

A gentle current of air ruffled the feathers of the bird. The woman held her breath as her son tossed it into the wind.

The creature stretched out its wings, and looked down on the woman and the boy. As if carried by their silent prayers it lifted, trembling, then glided smoothly in a wide circle high above the two of them, above the farm, above the entire valley.

The woman and her son never saw the eagle again. They never discovered where its heart directed it to go. They only knew it would never return to live the life of a chicken. Never again.

The most common mistake we make as parents is thinking one person can't make a difference. As the woman did in this African folktale, I would like to help you find the eagles inside your children. I would like to convince you that they are not chickens, and don't need to live their lives as if they were. I would like to support your saving their minds by learning to understand the unique patterns they use to think, learn, and communicate. I would like to help you find ways to support their flying beyond their belief that they can't fly.

3

Thinking About Thinking: How Your Child's Mind Works

> *"We will come to regard our children not as creatures to manipulate or to change, but rather as messengers from a world we once deeply knew, but which we have long since forgotten, who can reveal to us more about the secrets of life, and also our own lives, than our parents were ever able to do."*
>
> —Alice Miller

One of the biggest miseducations we suffer from is the assumption that all human beings use the same process for thinking. Obviously, we all think different thoughts. Not so obviously, we all have unique ways of thinking those thoughts. In school, little attention is given to *how* children think. It's usually assumed that everyone's mind operates in the same way as the teacher's does. In fact, there are six possible ways that we can "think." Understanding these patterns of processing information is crucial to finding the most effective ways to educate your child.

In this chapter, you will be presented with a flexible and simple framework to help you understand how thought moves through your child's mind. From there, we'll help you discover your child's natural thinking pattern.

Playing Our Own Tune

Our minds are much like the instruments of the orchestra. Musical instruments don't play music in the same way. They all make music, they are all instruments, but a violin is played in a very different way than a slide trombone.

What if your child, on the first day of school, came in carrying a violin? And what if your child's teacher came in carrying a flute, and a hidden assumption that all instruments must be played in the same fashion? The teacher might say something like, "All right, boys and girls, hold your instruments up to your lips and blow."

Your child, of course, would have great difficulty. He would be assigned special homework and told to try harder. You would, of course, try to help. You, having been taught that all instruments are played in the same manner, would hold your instrument, let's say a trumpet, up to your lips and blow. Johnny would do his level best to practice, but no sound would come out of his violin. Finally, he'd be tested, compared to all the other children with flutes and trumpets, harmonicas and trombones in the whole country. He would, of course, score in the lowest percentile, along with all the other kids who had violins, and drums.

Years of remedial "help" would help Johnny make some weird and feeble sounds, but his love of learning, self-worth, self-esteem, and basic trust in his instrument would be severely damaged.

The story does not have to end there. One day, Johnny's mother reads this little book and discovers that Johnny needs a bow to play his instrument. She finds a dusty one in the attic. She also notices that Johnny's uncle Sid has a very similar instrument and plays it quite well, and then . . . (Your imagination can take it from here!)

Changing Their Minds

I would like to share with you something of what I've learned about how minds process information so that you can understand the particular way your child uses his or her instrument to think, learn, and communicate. When I began to study hypnotherapy, I became aware that the mind digests thought by moving it through itself in three different ways, sometimes called states of consciousness: conscious, subconscious, and unconscious. Each state of mind has its particular functions in learning.

If we compare the learning process to the digestive system, the conscious state of mind is like the mouth: it's where learning begins, the doorway to the rest of the mental system, where information is taken in and chewed up, as the mind organizes how each detail will be metabolized. It is here that children's minds input, organize, prioritize, evaluate, and express information most easily. When a child cannot think in this mode, the world becomes a chaotic whirlpool.

It is commonly thought that children are learning and paying attention when they are thinking in this conscious state of mind, but that would be like saying that when we have food in our mouths we are eating. It is only the beginning of the learning/digestive process, and only a small portion of our brains are devoted to this function. Nature was not stupid. She gave us the ability to think in many ways for many different purposes.

When children are in the conscious state of mind, they are alert, with their attention turned to the outside world and what is being presented, sitting on the edge of their seats, watching everything that happens, hanging on every word.

To summarize, in the *conscious* state of mind:
- children feel most alert and awake
- they can easily pay attention to what's going on around them
- information seems most easily absorbed
- children express themselves comfortably in public
- they can be logical, organize details, stick to the point

The subconscious state of mind is where children sift things out. To continue the digestive metaphor, it is like the stomach: the place where things get churned around, and mixed together. The food isn't the same as it was when it entered your system, but it is not ready to be fully assimilated into your body yet either.

In this stage of the learning process, children pause to consider incoming information, weighing it carefully so they can notice how it fits with what they've already learned. It is here that they debate questions, wrestle with feelings, or see many differing viewpoints, all within themselves. This part of their minds is like a shuttle service which transports what they are receiving from the conscious mind back to the memory banks of the unconscious mind. It also transports what they have already learned from the storehouse of their unconscious minds to full consciousness so they can use it.

The subconscious mind is where children are aware of both the input they get from the outside world, and their inner frame of reference. It helps us move from alertness into deep relaxation, and from relaxation into active self-expression. Without this function, your mind would have to swallow everything whole.

To summarize, in the *subconscious* state of mind:
- children sort information
- they move between being alert and "spaced out"
- they can pay attention in and out at the same time
- they can get easily confused

The unconscious state is the one in which what children are learning is integrated with what they already know. Memories are brought to mind, and connections are made on a very deep level. This way of thinking is designed to make patterns by arranging and rearranging experience in many ways and communicating the way things could be. It is like the intestines of the mind, constantly changing the form of what has been digested, and connecting the nutrients to every part of the body. If the rational mind is devoted to organizing information into detailed meaning, this way of thinking is devoted to creating messages indirectly through dreams, symbols, imagery, analogy, in many directions at the same time. Here thought circles, and is concerned with the whole of a situation. Without the ability to think unconsciously, a child's life would be sterile, void of creativity and invention, isolated and boring.

To summarize, in the *unconscious* state of mind:
- children space out quite easily
- they think privately, intimately, shyly
- they perceive the whole of a situation rather than details
- they make creative connections

I use the symbols triangle, square, and circle to refer to each state of consciousness. The diagram on the next page puts these together. The arrow indicates the movement of thought inward as a mind receives information and processes it, and the movement outward as it produces, expresses, and transmits ideas.

In reality, we are each going through these three states of consciousness all the time, with split-second speed. They are being triggered constantly by the sensory information that comes our way.

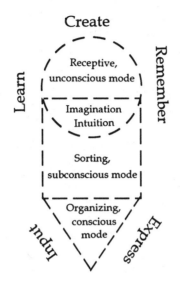

The Learning Loop

Let's go into the classroom for an example: Mrs. Jones is lecturing the students about fractions. Miguel seems to be right with it, poised on the edge of his seat, ready to ask and answer the next question. Alexandra, on the other hand, is drawing an intricate maze on the blue cover of her notebook. At the same time, Wai Lap is motionless, staring out the window, apparently not paying attention at all. When Mrs. Jones calls on him, he acts as if he just returned from Saturn on the space shuttle. She may get very frustrated, thinking that Miguel is the only one "getting" what she is trying to explain. She does not realize that each of these students is digesting differently what she is trying to teach, each is in a different state of consciousness. She also is not aware that the way she is presenting the material about fractions is stimulating those different ways of thinking.

Miguel, listening to Mrs. Jones, is *consciously* taking the information in, asking the questions he needs to understand what is being said. Alexandra, doodling while Mrs. Jones is speaking, is processing what she is hearing *subconsciously*. Her mind is sorting through it, trying to figure out how it is relevant to her, and related to her past experiences.

Wai Lap, staring out the window, is processing what Mrs. Jones is saying *unconsciously*. He may be thinking about a fraction of a pie he ate for dessert last night, or winning the swim meet last month by a fraction of a second. Or he might be imagining a kaleidoscope making patterns from fractions of glass.

Thinking About Thinking

Let's consider a thought to be like water. If you don't think about it very much, water is something you wash with or drink or use to brush your teeth. But if you consider a little more deeply, you'll realize that water changes form constantly, evaporating into clouds, pouring on your umbrella, rushing down a mountainside into the stream which feeds the spring behind your house. It's still water but it changes form.

In my experience, thought also changes form as it moves through the brain from one state of consciousness to another. Most of us who are familiar with computers understand that they use different kinds of "language" to process information, such as Fortran, Pascal, Basic, etc. What makes the human mind so fascinating is that it uses three different "languages" to think. I don't mean French, Hungarian, or Swahili. I am referring to visual, auditory, and kinesthetic imagery. In more detail, here is what each refers to:

Visual: Seeing the outer world, inner visual images, and creating what can be seen (reading, drawing, writing, designing, etc.);

Auditory: Listening to the outer world, inner voices and sounds, and expressing what can be heard (speaking, singing, chanting, music making, etc.);

Kinesthetic: Sensing from the outer world, inner feelings, or body sensations, and moving or doing in the world (touching, actions, experiencing, crafting etc.)

As a child's mind moves a thought from conscious, to subconscious, to unconscious, *it changes the language or software it is using to think in each way.* In Miguel's mind, for example, it began in auditory—he heard the description Mrs. Jones was giving him, and explained the meaning of what she was saying to himself (consciously and auditorily); his mind then changed her explanation into a picture as it sorted the information to make it relevant—he saw what she was saying (subconsciously and visually); and lastly, he spaced out for a moment or two as he lost track of the outside world and unconsciously remembered an experience he had of cutting up a pie (unconsciously and kinesthetically). If he stayed in that state of mind, it may have spun a web, connecting him to other kinesthetic feelings and actions, such as the first piece of pie he ever ate.

None of these is actually "the thought." What is important is *how the thought was moving through his mind.* Or wasn't. And could have. Perceptual processing is the phrase I use to describe this natural choreography of thinking. In all of our minds, each of the three perceptual channels (kinesthetic, auditory, and visual) is linked to one of three states of consciousness through which thought can move.

In lecturing to get her point across, Mrs. Jones is using her auditory channel. Since Miguel's mind uses the auditory channel to think consciously, the verbal explanations make him more alert. But Alexandra's auditory channel is linked to her subconscious, so that Mrs. Jones' words are inducing a sorting state of confusion in her. Our lost Wai Lap has an instrument whose unconscious mind is linked to the auditory channel, so all of the words trigger his unconscious thinking, the deepest part of his mind, causing him to seem "spaced out" and inattentive. (Which in a way *is* true because he's attending "in"!)

By exploring the ways children do simple everyday things, you can begin to understand the different ways their minds work. If three children walk into a new classroom, for instance, the first thing Jordan notices (her conscious mind) is what everyone is doing—kinesthetic channel. Thomas, on the other hand, is most attracted by what everyone is talking about first (his conscious mind using the auditory channel). Max initially looks around to see what's most interesting (consciously using the visual channel).

Let's consider how children get organized. In schools, it's discussed as if it were the same process for everyone. In fact, keeping track of details and prioritizing activities can be done in any number of ways: Jorge may be a child who needs to write down every homework assignment and refer to his list in order to get everything done, since his mind organizes things visually. Teri may like to get herself organized for her evening's work by talking on the phone and telling her friends what she has to do and in what order she's going to do it, since her mind organizes auditorily. Nanci may construct piles of her books and papers to work through one at a time until everything's completed, organizing the world kinesthetically.

Remembering is also not the same process for all children, whether they're recalling someone's phone number or a memory of their last birthday. Juanita sees the number she's dialing as though it's printed out on a small screen in her head (visually). Joshua hears a voice speak the numbers in order in his mind (auditorily). Leonard remembers by holding the phone in his hands and actually going through the motions of pushing the buttons or dialing in his mind (kinesthetically).

There is also a wide variety of ways children choose to express who they are and what they know. In one family, Donna may be the entertainer, keeping everyone laughing with jokes, songs, and stories at the dinner table; Rachel may be an athlete, always coming and going from practice and games, whether the sport is soccer, basketball or track; and Dale may be the artist, dabbling with paints, wood, or clay, displaying the latest masterpiece on the fridge or bookcase.

Education and Individual Differences

In the recent past, educators have been becoming more and more aware of the importance of differences in learning styles. Marie Carbo, Rita Dunn, Kenneth Dunn and others have been doing research on the subject since the late 1960's at St. John's University in New York. They have demonstrated conclusively that children learn in different ways, and their success in school depends upon being taught in a style that matches their learning style: "There is no best way; there are many different approaches, some of which are effective with some children and ineffective with others. Each youngster learns differently from every other one, and it is the match between how the learner learns and how the method teaches that determines who learns what—and how much."

Anne recalls when she first was exposed to learning styles: "As a teacher in the 1970's, I was excited about being trained to be aware of individual differences in students. I studied the 18 variables presented by Dunn and Dunn's research. I interviewed many of my students with the learning styles inventory based on their work. It was an interesting foundation, but even with all of this information, I was still at a loss as to how to apply what I was learning about each child and how to meet all of those needs at once in the daily life of the classroom. It was over-whelming to have that many variables to consider. So I went back to doing what I always did—teaching kids in what I thought was the best way—the way I learned."

Recently, information about learning styles is beginning to be utilized more widely in schools. Many approaches to under-standing individual differences include something about the fact that most of us have one sense we are most comfortable using in the learning process. It is not uncommon to hear about auditory, visual, and kinesthetic learners. The basic under-standing that these three perceptual preferences are at the core of learning differences is a giant step forward.

But it's only the first step. It's not enough to say that your child is a kinesthetic, auditory, or visual learner. It's necessary to understand the whole system of how your child digests expe-rience—how thought moves through his or her conscious, sub-conscious, and unconscious mind.

In the classroom we discussed before, if all you know about Wai Lap, for example, is that he is a kinesthetic learner, all you can do is give him a fraction puzzle to take apart and put together, which would probably keep him alert, but unless you know that his unconscious mind uses the auditory channel, you'd never understand why he spaced out when Mrs. Jones talked on and on.

Also, if Mrs. Jones didn't understand the whole system of how his mind worked, she might speak to him in a very critical tone of voice when he could not answer her questions. Because he is so sensitive to what he hears, this could damage his self-esteem, and he'd leave class thinking he was stupid, while she would chatter to the guidance counselor about how inattentive Wai Lap was!

The Six Personal Thinking Patterns

Children need to use all three channels to learn effectively. Our differences, then, are not a question of which mode our minds use to learn, but rather in what order we prefer to use them.

Information is most easily retained and retrieved when the process follows a certain sequence—when information is first received by our conscious minds, then sorted by our subconscious minds, and finally integrated by our unconscious minds. What makes one instrument different from another is the way each of the three states of consciousness is linked to the three channels of thought (visual, auditory, kinesthetic). There are six different combinations possible. These six are what I call personal thinking patterns, ways of *moving thought*, of metabolizing, digesting, processing experience.

△ Conscious	☐ Subconscious	○ Unconscious	
Visual	Auditory	Kinesthetic	(VAK)
Visual	Kinesthetic	Auditory	(VKA)
Auditory	Kinesthetic	Visual	(AKV)
Auditory	Visual	Kinesthetic	(AVK)
Kinesthetic	Visual	Auditory	(KVA)
Kinesthetic	Auditory	Visual	(KAV)

It is these patterns that are reflected in our different ways of doing things. It is these patterns that determine the most comfortable and effective way for each of us to learn something. It is these patterns that make Johnny's mind a violin and his mother's mind a trumpet.

I have no idea why one person's brain chooses a particular

pattern. But it seems that the most efficient and effective way for the human brain to function is by following a habitual perceptual track when it processes thoughts, for much the same reasons that we usually walk on sidewalks. At some point in a child's life, usually by first grade, one particular track becomes his or her preferred way of digesting experience. Not all or always, but usually. Changing back and forth would be as confusing for us as it might be if we were right-handed and left-handed every other day.

Even though certain children's minds appear to track in a particular pattern at a very young age, it is often difficult to determine perceptual preference until a child has matured neurologically. This varies with every child. Please stay curious as your child grows and changes, allowing your ideas about how he or she thinks also to grow and change.

Thinking Patterns from the Inside Out

In order for you to experience how these patterns work, I'd like to invite you to follow your own mind for a few minutes:

Notice how you think about something: not the content of your thoughts, but the process you use in thinking them. For example, if I ask you to think about the first time you experienced your child in the hospital, you might tell me, "It was seven o'clock in the morning on the 15th of November, 1985, and the sun was beginning to rise. I had only been in labor four hours when the doctor laid Melissa on my chest. She was the tiniest of my three kids, weighing just seven pounds, while her brothers had both been almost nine . . . . " That would be telling me the content of your thoughts.

If instead, however, you became aware that when you think of Melissa that first day, you first remember how light she felt in your arms and the warm feelings in your body, and then you hear the sounds of her cry and the doctor's voice, and then you get a clear picture of her tiny hands in the early morning light, that would be noticing how you think about that memory. Noticing the process means noticing how you think about the content.

At first, noticing in this way may seem as awkward as holding a baby seems when you first try. Be patient with yourself, breathe and ease into it. Just notice the process you use to think about the first time you held your child.

Here's an example. When I think about holding David for the first time, I get a visual, split-second flash of his face, how he looked wrapped up in a blanket. If I go a little deeper in my thoughts, I remember the sounds of his gurgling and singing to him on my shoulder. This triggers remote feelings of fullness and warmth as he snuggled into my neck.

Thus, my brain uses all three perceptual modes to "think," but visual recall is what comes first, and what seems most like organized, conscious reality to me. Auditory dialogue and descriptions are right below the surface in my subconscious thinking, and take a little longer to access. Feelings, touch, movement, and actions, although very profound, come from so deep in my unconscious mind that I do not usually "think" of them. My mind habitually tracks in this Visual-Auditory-Kinesthetic pattern most of the time.

Which of the six patterns would you guess your mind uses to process information? In working with your own thinking pattern, you may discover more about how you process information than you've ever been consciously aware of before.

Building Bridges Across the Communication Gap

Knowing more about how both you and your children's minds work can transform how you relate to them. Understanding personal thinking patterns invites you to respect and appreciate each other as whole persons. It supports your curiosity without considering a particular behavior as indicative of a problem or a weakness. It provides specific, understandable ways to respond. It invites you to notice what works as well as what doesn't.

Here's an example: A few months ago, I was being interviewed on the phone for a late-night radio program. There were fifteen minutes to go when a caller from a nearby suburb captured my attention.

"I've been listening to you for the past forty-five minutes and I decided to call and ask you something." His voice was deep and gruff, his words came in a burst.

"I've been beating up my son a lot to try and get him to listen to me. Whenever I try to tell him something important, he just stands there, staring at me, goofy-like, giving me the silent treatment. I thought it was because he was being a wise-ass, but after hearing you, I'm not so sure."

I took a deep breath. What could I say that might make a difference? I asked him to describe everything he knew about how his son's mind worked.

"Well, after listening to you, I think he's one of those visual/kinesthetic kinds, 'cause he loves to doodle and can't talk unless he uses his hands like a windmill. He just watches me do anything and then he can do it. But when I try to explain something to him, he looks real annoyed or `out to lunch.'"

After asking him a few more questions, we both agreed his son's mind probably used the VKA pattern. There was no question in either of our minds that the father's mind used the opposite pattern, AKV.

"That's what I was afraid you were going to say. So I've been hitting him all this time for something that isn't his fault?"

I suggested that if he had understood this before, he wouldn't have been hitting his son, so it wasn't his fault either.

"Well, now that I know, what do I do?"

We talked about how important it was for his son to be touched with love. I suggested that when he needed the boy to listen to him, he put his arm around his shoulders and go for a walk with him, allowing their eyes to look wherever they wanted. Movement and action could bridge them together in their common kinesthetic channel. A shoulder-to-shoulder kind of communication would maximize the possibility of his son being able to pay attention to all of his words and respond.

I received a letter from him a month later. He reported that he hadn't hit his son once since our late night conversation, that his son did, indeed, listen when they went for walks, and that he was learning as much about how his own mind worked as he was about his son's.

Putting It All Together

Finding your child's pattern is like a bit like a cut-and-paste puzzle or selecting a banquet in a Chinese restaurant: choose one from the conscious column, one from the subconscious, and one from the unconscious column and you have your personal thinking pattern or, if you're totally confused, Moo Goo Gai Pan! The chapters that follow will assist you in the process. For now, you are cordially invited to stay deliciously curious!

In finding out how your child's mind works, you may begin to understand behaviors that have been puzzling or irritating to you in the past. I hope that your increased understanding will also deepen your compassion for your children in learning situations where the teaching style does not match their thinking pattern and motivate you to find ways to help them get their learning needs met more effectively. Their uniqueness is, after all, our true abundance.

Homework

Just because you're there and I'm here, on different sides of the page, doesn't mean you have to let the learning in this book passively happen to you. Join me now, by thinking about something: What do you want to learn about how your children learn that you don't know now?

4

Identifying Your Child's Thinking Pattern

"There is no such thing as a genius. Some of us are less damaged than others."
—Buckminster Fuller

Every parent knows about individual differences. If you have more than one child, it's not uncommon to make comparisons such as "Sally was a climber, but Justin can be content to sit and watch the world go by." In your everyday life with your children, you notice the little things—the traits that make them endearing and those that drive you crazy. You notice that Ted can't ever seem to sit still, that Rosita is always asking "Why?," that Katie is so neat and tidy, that Reggie is the quiet one in the family, or that Lana has always been good with her hands. These simple, everyday things that make each child stand out in your mind are the details that will help you understand how he or she learns.

In this chapter, you'll learn to identify your child's thinking pattern. We will provide you with questions, activities to do by yourself and with your child, a list of familiar characteristics, a comparative chart, and an inventory of common behaviors. Chapters 5-10 explore each of the six patterns in greater depth, providing detailed behavior profiles and suggestions for communicating more effectively with your child and helping him or her with schoolwork at home. The final chapters offer information you can use to begin a dialogue about all of this with your child's teacher.

For now, consider yourself a detective, gathering many clues, digging deep into what you already know about your child, and becoming aware of behaviors or traits you might have taken for granted. We think you'll find this a fascinating adventure, one that will leave you saying, "Oh, so *that's* why!"

What Do You Already Know?

You as a parent know more about your children than anyone else does. You've been with them as they learned to walk and talk and read and write. You've watched them, listened to them, and encouraged them as they've begun to explore and develop their talents and interests. You've helped them cope with their frustrations in learning, relating, and communicating.

The place to start in identifying your child's pattern is with what you already know about how he or she learns. Take some time now to document, on a tape recorder or paper, everything you can think of. Use the following suggestions to guide you, but feel free to expand your thinking beyond them:

• *Think of several experiences you've had with your child as he or she learned something new. For example, how did she learn to swim? Did he want you to show him how to do each stroke first and then talk through it while he tried it for himself? Did she just jump in and ask questions later? How did he learn to play baseball or drive a car?*

• *Make a list of your child's interests. What is he or she intensely curious about?*

• *What school subjects are easy for your child? Which ones give her trouble? What are his strengths as a student? Where does he need extra support? Consider music, art, home economics, shop, and sports as well as reading, writing, math, spelling, social studies, and science.*

Allow your mind to float with these questions. Go away from them and come back. You may be surprised by what memories bubble to the surface that you haven't thought about in years.

Your Child's Thinking Pattern

The simplest way to determine your children's thinking patterns involves paying attention when they speak and listen, learn to dance or play sports, read or draw. This will help you discover where the auditory, kinesthetic, and visual channels are in their patterns.

What follows is a list of the characteristics you are likely to encounter with each possible combination of perceptual channels and states of mind. Notice which of these sections (ideally, one from the conscious mind group, one from subconscious mind, and one from unconscious mind) remind you most of your child. Consider these as clues to help you recognize his or her thinking pattern.

Please do not expect your child to fit any of our descriptions exactly; no one does. Each pattern has a set of essential behaviors and qualities which most people with that pattern manifest fairly consistently, habitually, and comfortably, but we are *all* exceptions to the rules. There are wide variations among people of the same pattern—there are VAKs who are athletic, AKVs who read a lot, and VKAs who speak eloquently. Therefore, as you move through this process, look for the *overall* tendencies and don't get too caught up in specifics.

If your child's *conscious mind* uses the *kinesthetic channel*, he or she:
learns and remembers physical things easily
enjoys athletic competition

does things in an organized way
describes body sensations and feelings without hesitation
is more alert when moving or using hands

If your child's *conscious mind* **uses the** *auditory channel,* **he or she:**
learns and remembers things that are heard easily
is naturally comfortable speaking in front of people
uses detailed and organized vocabulary
is more alert when speaking

If your child's *conscious mind* **uses the** *visual channel,* **he or she:**
learns and remembers things that are seen easily
is naturally comfortable being seen, writing, showing ideas
organizes visually by making lists, writing things down,
    making things look neat
is very aware of visual details
is more alert when showing or writing something

◆ ◆ ◆

If your child's *subconscious mind* **uses the** *kinesthetic channel,* **he or she:**
sorts by trying options or doing something in many different
    ways
pays attention outward by moving, inward by feeling
can feel and move simultaneously
often feels pulled in two directions

If your child's *subconscious mind* **uses the** *auditory channel,* **he or she:**
sorts by talking things through out loud

pays attention outward by speaking, inward by listening

can talk and listen simultaneously

dialogues both sides of a conversation inside

If your child's *subconscious mind* uses the *visual channel*, he or she:

sorts by writing, drawing, visualizing options

pays attention outward by looking, inward by visualizing

can see out and see inner images simultaneously with eyes
   open

sees things from two perspectives at the same time

◆ ◆ ◆

If your child's *unconscious mind* uses the *kinesthetic channel*, he or she:

"spaces out" when touched or moving in a set way

is shy and/or private when expressing through movement
   or touch

finds it easier to express an overall feeling than pinpoint
   specific physical sensations

can easily forget how to do something physical

If your child's *unconscious mind* uses the *auditory channel*, he or she:

"spaces out" when listening to too many words

is shy and/or private when talking, particularly to strangers
   or in groups

can easily forget what was said, names of things or titles;
   remembers tone of voice

If your child's *unconscious mind* uses the *visual channel*, he or she:

spaces out when looking at something for too long

may be shy when expressing through writing or drawing

finds it easier to remember the big picture than visual details
can easily forget what has been read or seen

◆ ◆ ◆

Whether you've already noticed your child's pattern or
simply have a mass of clues but no overall guess, I suggest that
you use your mind much like a zoom lens as you continue this
process. Go back and forth between paying attention to detailed
behavior and taking in the whole of who you know your child
to be. Avoid zeroing in on one characteristic or one channel and
making an assumption about a pattern.

Move between what you read here and your present-day
experience of your child. Involve your child in this process, too.
Ask him or her to teach you something. It could be something he
is very interested in at the moment, like how to dribble a soccer
ball or how to do an algebra problem. Or have her teach you
something very basic, such as how to tie your shoes. What
channels does she use first? second? last or not at all? We teach
most comfortably in the same way that we learn.

You might want to think of the process of identifying your
child's pattern as similar to buying a sweatshirt: imagine that
there are six different styles. At some point, you will choose one
and try it on your child. Take it home and have him wear it for
a while. Observe him in it and reserve the right to take it back
and try another if the first one really doesn't fit.

Be patient. Above all, trust yourself. There is no right way to
do this. Allow yourself some freedom and have fun with it. You
may find the investigation so interesting that 'figuring out' your
child's pattern becomes less important than just staying curious.

The inventory of common behaviors included on the following pages may help you determine your child's pattern by
expanding and organizing your observations. As you go through
it, we'd like to invite you to let go of old assumptions and

judgments you might have about how your child behaves and why. The process is meant to give you new ways to consider his or her frustrating, puzzling, and fascinating behaviors.

THINKING PATTERNS INVENTORY

Directions: For each question, choose the answer that's most true and make a check mark in the appropriate column on page 61. If more than one option is given, choose both. For example, if the answer to question 1 is "a," make a checkmark in both the AKV and AVK columns. After you've answered all the questions, count up how many check marks you have in each column. The one with the most is probably your child's pattern. To help confirm this, read the charts that begin on page 63.

From what you can readily observe:

1. How would you describe how your child talks?
    a. Words pour out, in logical order,
       all the time, without hesitation;
       has an excellent vocabulary   AKV, AVK
    b. May be self-conscious or shy about
       speaking in groups   VKA, KVA
    c. Uses many metaphors and images ("It's
       like a cyclone, a blue funnel,
       a whirling top")   VAK, KAV
    d. Talks mostly about actions, feelings,
       what's happening   KAV
    e. Makes hand motions before words, must use
       hands or movement to find words   VKA, KAV
    f. Talks in circles, asks endless questions   VKA, KVA

2. How would you describe your child's eye contact?
a. Maintains steady, persistent eye contact VAK, VKA
b. "Eye shy," uncomfortable with eye
   contact for more than a few seconds,
   looks away frequently AKV, KAV
c. Keeps steady contact, but blinks or
   twitches if sustained AVK, KVA
d. Eyes glaze over if listening too long VKA, KVA

3. How would you describe your child's handwriting?
a. Neat and legible VAK, VKA
b. Difficult to read AVK, KVA
c. Immature, sometimes messy,
   may have difficulty forming letters AKV, KAV

4. What does your child remember most easily?
a. What's been said, jokes, lyrics, names
   of people, titles; memorizes by saying
   something repeatedly AKV, AVK
b. What's been seen or read, people's faces,
   how something looks; memorizes by
   writing something repeatedly VAK, VKA
c. What's been done or experienced, the feel
   or smell of something; memorizes by
   doing something repeatedly KVA, KAV

5. How would you describe your child's physical needs and skills?
a. Is constantly in motion, wiggly,
   needs freedom to move KVA, KAV
b. Can sit still easily for long periods AVK, VAK
c. Can feel awkward or get easily frustrated
   when first learning physical activity AVK, VAK

    d. Learns physical skills easily   KVA, KAV

6. How does your child respond to touch?

    a. Tends to be shy about physical contact   AVK, VAK

    b. Likes to touch and be touched frequently   KVA, KAV

    c. Touches after initial contact   AKV, VKA

7. How does your child express his or her feelings?

    a. Very private about feelings   VAK

    b. Feelings seem right beneath the surface   AKV, VKA

    c. Expresses feelings easily   AKV, KAV

    d. Expresses reasons for feelings easily   AVK

    e. Almost impossible to put feelings
into words   KVA

8. Under what conditions does your child "space out?"

    a. With too much visual detail, being shown
something, or questions about what they see   AKV, KAV

    b. With too many words, verbal explanations,
or questions about what they have heard   VKA, KVA

    c. With too many choices of what to do, being
touched, or questions about how they feel   AVK, VAK

9. What is your child's most frustrating behavior?

    a. Can't sit still or stay put   AKV, KAV

    b. Communicates first physically,
with slap or push   KAV

    c. "Shows off"   VAK

    d. Wisecracks, is "fresh" verbally   AKV, AVK

    e. Gets sullen or withdraws   VKA, KVA

    f. Interrupts, talks incessantly   AKV, AVK

    g. Whines, complains, "yeah-but's"   VKA

For more information, ask your child the following:

10. What do you remember most easily after seeing a movie, a TV program, or reading:
- a. What the people and the scenes looked like   VAK, VKA
- b. What was said or how the music sounded   AKV, AVK
- c. What happened or how the characters felt   KVA, KAV

11. What's the first thing you do to remember someone's phone number?
- a. Say it to myself or hear it in my head   AKV, AVK
- b. See the phone or the numbers in my head   VAK, VKA
- c. Feel myself picking up the phone
     and dialing   KVA, KAV

12. What's the thing you remember most easily about people you just met?

- a. What you did with them or how they felt   KVA, KAV
- b. How they looked   VAK, VKA
- c. Their name or what they said   AKV, AVK

13. What's the scariest, hardest for you to take?
- a. Mean, hurtful words   VKA, KVA
- b. Poking, invasive touch   AVK, VAK
- c. Nasty looks   AKV, KAV

14. How do you put something together?
- a. I read the directions and then do it.
     Telling me confuses me.   VKA
- b. I read the directions, ask questions,
     then talk to myself as I do it.   VAK
- c. I work with the pieces, then ask questions
     if I need to. I never read directions.   KAV
- d. I work with the pieces, look at the diagram,

then ask questions.   KVA

e. I have someone tell me, then show me how,
then I try it.   AVK

f. I have someone tell me how to do it, then I try
it. I only read directions as a last resort.   AKV

15. What's most important when you decide which clothes to wear?

a. How they feel, how comfortable they are,
the texture   KVA, KAV

b. The colors, how they look on me, how they
go together   VAK, VKA

c. An idea of what's me, the brand name,
what the clothes say about me   AKV, AVK

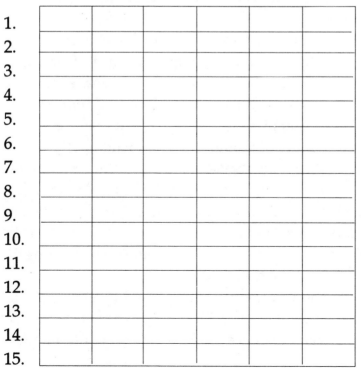

	AKV	AVK	KAV	KVA	VKA	VAK
1.						
2.						
3.						
4.						
5.						
6.						
7.						
8.						
9.						
10.						
11.						
12.						
13.						
14.						
15.						

Charts of Pattern Differences

The charts that begin on the following page give you brief descriptions of the most obvious characteristics of each of the six patterns and refine the ideas you may have about your child's pattern from the inventory.

Understanding How Your Child Understands

I'd like to share an example with you of how knowing her child's thinking pattern helped a mother get through what seemed like an impossible communication gap.

Sally is beside herself with frustration. She crosses and recrosses her white-stockinged legs, then fluffs her newly-permed sandy hair. Her seven-year-old son, Richard, is running haphazardly around her, throwing a Nerf basketball into a plastic hoop mounted on the door. Her voice is nasal, almost whining, and she speaks as rapidly as Richard moves in his red high-top sneakers.

"I have to tell you, he's been tested and the school psychologist insists he is hyperactive and oppositional. They demand that I put him on Ritalin. He just will not behave. I am so frustrated I don't know what else to do. I've read some studies in my nursing journal that say there are possible side effects to the drug, but the school wouldn't recommend anything that would hurt him, would they?" She touches an immaculate handkerchief to her nose. "He has to learn to pay attention. When I engage him in a conversation about it, he just goes deaf and dumb. Last week, I took him for a walk in the woods and he was actually violent. He picked up a stick and started hitting the beautiful poplar trees we walked past.

"His father and I have joint custody, but I don't talk to him, so I don't know how it is when Richard's over at his house. He drives a trailer truck. I believe unless we attend to this immedi-

	AKV	**AVK**
Language Characteristics	Interacts with others easily by talking. Has extensive vocabulary. Speaks with lots of feeling and rhythm. Likes to tell others what to do (natural leaders).	Interacts with others easily by talking. Has extensive vocabulary. Speaks logically about facts, ideas, concepts. Likes talking with adults and older children.
Visual Characteristics	Is "eye-shy"—cannot maintain eye contact. Sees whole picture. Makes simple drawings. Has messy handwriting with unique style.	Makes steady eye contact--may blink, flutter, twitch. Can pay attention to "big picture" and details at same time. Can turn images around in his/her mind. Has hard-to-read handwriting.
Physical Characteristics	Has pent-up energy right below the surface. Enjoys sports—good coaches, athletes. May be tentative about touch at first.	May have sketchy sense of his/her body. May be awkward, easily frustrated by physical activities. Prefers free-form activities (running, swimming) to competitive sports. Is shy about touch, private about feelings.
Learning Strengths and Challenges	Learns easily through discussion and lecture. Learns well with hands-on approach. Can have difficulty with reading, writing, spelling. Can learn to speak languages by ear.	Learns easily through discussion and lecture. Learns well through reading. Has difficulty with hands-on learning activities, sports. Can learn languages easily by ear and by reading.
"Spaces Out"	With too many things to look at, questions about what s/he sees.	With touch, questions about how how s/he feels.
Typical Trouble	Interrupts others. Can be "wisecracker"—sarcastic, fresh, kids around too much, hurts others with his/her words.	Interrupts others. Monopolizes conversations. Asks many "Why?" questions.
Frustrations	Has difficulty feeling satisfied when trying to make visions into reality.	Has difficulty putting feelings into words. Has difficulty learning physical skill without words or visuals to follow.
Natural Gifts	Is visionary thinker—has many great ideas. Wants to inspire others.	Is great communicator—loves to exchange ideas. Wants to help.

	KVA	**KAV**
Language Characteristics	Is usually soft-spoken. Speaks concisely. Speaks rarely in groups. May take a long time to find words, with big pauses between them. Needs silence to find words.	Enjoys talking about personal experiences. Is good at teaching activities, explaining movement. Likes to tell stories. Uses hand motions to help find his/her words.
Visual Characteristics	Makes steady eye contact—may blink, flutter, twitch. Can pay attention to "big picture" and visual details at same time. Can turn images around in his/her mind and see them from many angles. Can have hard-to-read handwriting.	Is "eye-shy"—cannot maintain eye contact. Can take in the "whole" of something with a glance. Organizes by making piles. Is rarely aware of visual images. May have messy handwriting with unique style.
Physical Characteristics	Interacts most easily with others by doing something together or making physical contact. Loves to be active, likes to move, do. Has smooth, graceful energy. Is usually well-coordinated, natural athlete. Likes competitive sports. Likes to touch and be touched. Learns physical skills easily.	Interacts most easily with others by doing something together or making physical contact. Is constantly moving, doing. Has huge amounts of physical energy. Is usually well-coordinated, natural athlete. Likes competitive sports. Likes to touch and be touched.
Learning Strengths and Challenges	Learns easily with hands-on or experiential approaches. Can be good reader, if taught through experience, not phonics. Has difficulty with oral reading and reports. Has difficulty concentrating in lecture classes or participating in discussions.	Learns physical skills easily. Learns easily with hands-on or experiential approaches. Can learn well from discussions about relevant subjects. Can have difficulty with reading, writing, spelling.
"Spaces Out"	With long verbal explanations, questions about what s/he thinks or what s/he's heard.	With many things to look at, or questions about what s/he sees.
Typical Trouble	Can get sullen and withdrawn.	Can get "hyperactive," has difficulty sitting still, fidgets.
Frustrations	Has great difficulty expressing feelings in words.	Has difficulty finding positive outlets for physical energy.
Natural Gifts	Is great lover of nature, especially animals. Has many dissimilar interests (eg., drawing and ice hockey). Wants to unite dissimilar elements.	Is great "doer"—loves to take action, get things done. Wants what s/he does to be useful to others.

	VAK	**VKA**
Language Characteristics	Speaks with feeling and emphasis. Loves to tell stories, explain, persuade others. Talks out loud to sort ideas and make decisions. Uses fillers like "um," "like," or "you know." Likes to convince people with words.	Speaks from personal experience in circling way. Must use hands or move to speak. May take a long time to find words, with long pauses between them. Speaks rarely in groups.
Visual Characteristics	Connects with others most easily with eye contact. Shows what s/he feels on his/her face. Keeps organized with lists, notes. Likes visual order. Has neat, legible handwriting.	Connects with others most easily with eye contact. Feels what s/he sees. Keeps organized with lists, notes. Needs visual order to think clearly. Has neat, legible handwriting.
Physical Characteristics	Can sit still for long periods. May be awkward, easily frustrated by physical activities. Has sketchy sense of his/her body; needs to close eyes to feel sensation. Is shy about touch, private about feelings. Prefers free-form activities (running, swimming) to competitive sports.	Has pent-up energy right below the surface. Learns sports easily, good athlete. Can tell what s/he feels in body quite easily with eyes open. May be tentative about touch. Likes organized, competitive sports. May confuse others' feelings and sensations with his/her own.
Learning Strengths and Challenges	Is avid reader—learns to read easily. Learns well by reading and talking about, or teaching others. Writes, spells, proofreads well. Has difficulty with hands-on learning activities, structured physical skill lessons.	Can be good reader, if taught words by sight rather than phonics. Learns easily by watching and then doing, without words and taking notes. Writes, spells, proofreads well. Has difficulty with oral reading and reports, concentrating in lectures or participating in discussion classes.
"Spaces Out"	With touch, questions about what s/he wants to do or how s/he feels.	With long verbal explanations, questions about what s/he thinks or what s/he's heard.
Typical Trouble	Shows off. Can be overly helpful to make good impression.	Can be whiner and complainer. Can go along with the crowd too much.
Frustrations	Has difficulty making time estimates.	Has difficulty thinking for self.
Natural Gifts	Is great teacher—loves to show and tell. Wants to illuminate.	Is great partner, works well with others. Wants to create networks between people, make connections.

ately, Richard will grow up to be . . . just like him."

Sally, the classroom teacher, and the school psychologist all think there is something wrong with Richard. Sally has come to me expecting to have what is wrong fixed, changed, "therapized." But the difficulties her son is experiencing are not because there is something "wrong" with him (or her)—they are primarily due to a lack of understanding about how his mind receives and communicates experience.

Sally's pattern is AVK. Her brain organizes information through words, sorts and deals with confusion visually, and integrates what comes in from the outside world most slowly and creatively through feelings and movement. Her son Richard's brain uses exactly the opposite thinking pattern: consciously organizing through movement and action and unconsciously creating through words and voice tones (KVA). So, when he is in motion, she feels confused and begins to get scared. If he strikes trees with a stick, a normal seven-year-old behavior, she imagines he is violent. Spoken words, which are her strength, are his downfall. They trigger his unconscious mind, causing him to "space out." She and his teachers interpret that as daydreaming and not paying attention. When he tries to pay attention by moving around, attempting to come forward to his kinesthetic channel, they say he is hyperactive and needs to be drugged. There is some truth to the description that he is oppositional—his mind works in a way that is the opposite of many school personnel—and his mother!

Instead of creating a remedial program, I taught Sally and Richard how his mind works. Understanding that moving helps him to pay attention has enabled her to feel comfortable with his jiggling energy and helped his teachers design an appropriate school program based on concrete, hands-on experience.

Sally is learning to touch Richard when she talks to him. She gives him physical work around the house to raise his sense of self-worth, and has made visual charts and cartoons of what she had previously been telling him over and over to no avail. A gymnastics program provides him with success experiences as well as a way to channel his exuberant physical energy. And I am teaching Richard to recognize when he feels too full of words and how to signal that he is overwhelmed. Both his performance at school and his relationship with his mother are improving greatly.

Still Not Sure?

Spending time with your children and being curious are the best guides you can have in understanding how their minds work. The in-depth descriptions of each pattern that begin with Chapter 5 will help you become more sure about your guesses.

Identifying your child's pattern is not meant to be the end of the process, but the beginning. Please use the information and suggestions in the following chapters to guide your child toward greater satisfaction in learning and fuller trust in his or her mind.

Homework

Here's a interesting way to integrate what you've learned in this chapter: *Remembering that these patterns are meant to be nests and not pigeon holes, use this chapter as a reference guide and guess the pattern of your friends, neighbors, the person who delivers packages, and the writer of "Cheers!"*

5

The Leaders of the Pack: AKV

"We are all so different largely because we all have different combinations of intelligences. If we recognize this, I think we will have at least a better chance of dealing appropriately with the many problems that we face in the world."
—Howard Gardner

Auditory-Kinesthetic-Visual

Easiest Way to Learn: Hear/Experience/See
Easiest Way to Express: Say/Do/Show

Pattern Snapshot

Meet the AKVs, highly verbal kids with lots of energy. They love to lead, to take charge, to tell everyone else what to do. They speak clearly and almost incessantly, with a lot of energy, feeling, and rhythm to their words. Even when they are not speaking, they are usually making sounds, whether whistling, mumbling, or creating sound effects for every situation.

Listening is not easy for AKVs and they may interrupt others often, especially if they are feeling a lot of excitement. AKVs have immense physical energy bubbling right beneath the surface.

Most AKVs are pile makers and collectors of small treasures. Children with this pattern are "eye-shy"—they cannot maintain steady eye contact. They generally have lots of "big ideas" and they often experience frustration and dissatisfaction when they can't or don't know how to make their dreams come true. Though they have extensive speaking vocabularies, learning to read and write can be a slow, laborious task.

Language Characteristics

AKV children are masterful in their use of language from a very young age. They love to discuss, argue, or debate anything, ask questions, tell jokes, and make plays on words. They understand and make verbal inferences easily and respond quickly to spoken questions. AKVs can often do impressions, taking on accents and voice tones with remarkable accuracy. They can be wisecrackers, who are sarcastic, fresh, or "kid" around verbally. They usually have distinctive, one-of-a-kind voices.

AKV children will remember what is said to them and often can repeat what they've heard word for word, in tape recorder fashion. This includes poetry, song lyrics, rhymes, and jokes as well as commercial jingles, profanity, and family "secrets." Subtleties of meaning and pronunciation are often important to them.

These children have strong feelings and opinions which they express easily. They tend to yell or argue when they are angry. Hand gestures usually follow their words and punctuate what they are expressing. AKVs can get their feelings hurt easily by what is said to them, but they often don't realize the power of their words to wound others.

Physical Characteristics

AKVs seem to have an endless supply of physical energy which is not easily released. While their bodies express how they feel, their faces rarely show it and can look almost flat most of the time. AKVs are sometimes eloquently coordinated and can easily learn physical moves if given verbal instructions. They generally like to participate in sports and are also good coaches; they can easily find the words to teach someone else what to do.

AKV children need to move a lot unless they are engrossed in what they are hearing, seeing, or saying. They get uncomfortable quickly if confined to a desk or small space for any length of time, especially if they are asked to deal with a lot of written material. Teachers in traditional school settings frequently tell AKVs to sit down and be quiet.

Children with the AKV pattern are fairly independent; they are good at taking action on their own. In fact, they need to feel at least somewhat in charge of what they do and how they do it. They learn to make choices by being given options, even with the most routine, daily tasks.

AKVs typically feel pulled in two directions when they are trying to make a decision about something. They often come to a conclusion by talking about each possibility and then trying each one out, noticing how they feel. This may make them seem scattered at times, as if they can't make up their minds. An AKV teenager deciding between two after-school waitressing jobs, for example, would do well to talk to each employer at length and visit each restaurant, if not try out both, before choosing the one that will work best for her.

AKVs can be a little tentative about physical contact. They often are more open to touch with a new person in their life after they have talked to him or her for a while.

Visual Characteristics

AKVs often develop a unique style of organizing their possessions. Frequently, they create order by making piles which are out in full view. Things do not have to be neat; they generally can live with visual clutter. AKV kids tend to be collectors; they want to keep everything that is visually interesting to them, in addition to everything they've ever written, drawn, or received in writing.

Their visual images tend to be simple, unique, and profound, capturing the whole feeling of what they are trying to express when drawing or painting. They may have difficulty with handwriting; the results may look "immature" and somewhat messy. AKVs often insist on their own penmanship style. Perfection in visual form is often their goal and they can get frustrated when they don't achieve it.

These children are shy about making eye contact while listening. They also will look away or blink frequently while talking. AKVs are usually very particular about the visual images they choose—movies, television shows, and room decorations— since they are deeply influenced by what they see. A nasty look from someone else can make a lasting impression on them. They may take on the physical style or rhythm of something they have seen, such as characters in cartoons, television programs, or movies.

AKVs will space out when they are given too much visual detail to look at, especially if it is not something they have chosen for themselves. Their eyes may also get distant when they are asked a question about what they see.

AKVs can be visionary dreamers. Many of them have vivid imaginations which overflow with new ideas about how things could be. However, they often have trouble feeling satisfied when they can't quickly turn their ideas into reality.

Learning to read can be a tedious task for AKVs. They may have difficulty decoding words visually and remembering even simple sight words. Their speaking vocabulary is often considerably more extensive than their reading vocabulary. AKV children love to be read to, preferring to listen rather than to read themselves. Typically, they read infrequently, but when they do, they get deeply immersed in what they read. For some, once the basic skill is learned, reading can become a pleasure-filled imaginative escape, a favorite way to "travel."

AKV Portrait

Anne remembers, "One of my students in fifth grade was Jonathan, who mumbled incessantly to himself in a peculiar, articulate way. At the time, I would have said he had a `quick mind.' I loved to talk with Jonathan one-to-one and was often surprised at the clarity of what he had to say. He was comfortable in adult conversation and always had a joke or an interesting question waiting for me.

"Jonathan seemed powered by some internal combustion, always doing, always thinking about something. The other kids thought he was kind of an oddball. He kept to himself a lot, except in the spring, when he was pitcher, captain, and student coach of the fifth grade baseball team."

"On the academic side, things were difficult for Jonathan. Written all over his cumulative folder were teachers' comments and test scores that showed he had a lot of `potential.' In fact, in fourth grade, he had been nominated for the gifted and talented program, but his teacher had vetoed his participation. Jonathan had a tough time getting even the simplest reading and math assignments in at all, much less on time. He seemed to have difficulty concentrating in class; he would promise to make up for lost time at home, but the assignments rarely made it back to school. Jonathan's desk was constantly overflowing into the aisle, with an `organization' only he understood. How could we offer him an academic `extra' when he couldn't seem to handle the basics?

"In fifth grade, his parents and I decided to let him try the gifted program for one semester. The teacher, Mrs. Noble, was a very creative but no-nonsense person who liked Jonathan and supported our decision. In the course of their unit on quantum physics, she discovered his `secret' talent for drawing and painting. This seemed to have a dramatic effect on his self-esteem and on his school performance.

"Jonathan asked me if he could bring a stool from home to use at his desk; he said he could learn better if it felt more like a drawing table. He was so excited when I said yes. He chose to put his new seat by the window because of the `creative light' he said came in there. Within a week, he began toting a bright red fishing tackle box, which contained his art supplies. I was amazed when he showed me that every pencil, marker, and paint brush had its own place. The pride and attention he brought to his artwork began to spill over into his daily assignments. He would complete work more efficiently so he would have free time to draw. I'll never forget the day he actually asked to stay in from recess to clean his desk!

"Jonathan found an important source of internal motivation in his own creativity. The options and encouragement we provided as parents and teachers went a long way, too, in helping him find his desire to succeed academically."

Communicating with AKV Children

Supporting Their Auditory Channel

AKV kids want to be listened to, talked with, and appreciated for their ideas. Set aside time just to talk. Help them to remember their everyday or special experiences by encouraging them to tell you what they said, heard, did, or felt. Try "What did you talk about in school today?" for starters rather than "What did you do?" Ask them occasionally what they've been thinking about or what they are curious about. Let them know you are listening by asking them follow-up questions or commenting specifically on what you've found interesting in what they've told you.

It helps AKVs listen better if you give them a one sentence introduction to your conversation. For example, "I'd like to talk with you about how things are going in science class." Then, ask a question or invite theirs. Discuss things with these children rather than lecture to them, dictate to them, or give them the silent treatment. If there is a choice to be made or something you are considering, like where to go for the family vacation or whether to get a new pet, ask for their opinion and include them in the decision-making process. Let them know you value their thinking.

AKVs appreciate clear, straight-forward explanations. Relate a new or up-coming experience to past experience. They also love humor: use funny voices, accents, or jokes to get your point across, even in emotionally-charged discussions. Have patience for AKVs' need to repeat what they have heard. They may have to tell the same story to three different people. They are making sure they've got it and that's how you will know they have taken in what's been said. Invite them to tell what you want them to remember to someone else—a friend, their teddy bear, or their younger sibling.

These children have a finely-tuned understanding of verbal language. Always assume that they have heard and understood you. Don't be afraid to use sophisticated language. Most of them love the challenge of understanding new words; most will ask you what an unfamiliar word means. Notes Anne, "When my son Brian was two, I told him one night that I was `frustrated' with something I was making for dinner. Two days later, I heard this little voice saying `I'm sooo frustrated!' as he was trying to drag his two big teddy bears over the side of his crib." Honor AKVs' verbal abilities as a strength and help them develop it well.

Help these children learn courtesy in speaking; they tend to be interrupters. Help them understand that they can't be listened to all the time. Remind them not to interrupt and don't interrupt them. Let them know what the specific limits are around your availability. Tell them specifically when you will be off the phone or when you can give them your undivided attention. Encourage them to record on tape or paper what they want to share or encourage them to find someone else to talk to when your attention is not available. Let them know when you need quiet, and respect the times when they ask for it, too.

Develop interactive listening skills with your AKV kids: ask them to tell you what you've said before they speak, so you know they are listening all the way through.

Set limits around the content and tone of their voices. You might say, "I want you to express how you are feeling with me, but I need you to use a respectful tone. I can't listen when you get so bossy." Be aware that they can pick up your feelings from your tone of voice quite easily as well.

Supporting Their Kinesthetic Channel

AKVs' sense of self-esteem will be enhanced if they have opportunities to be in charge of what they do and how they do it. These children easily navigate with rules that they have had a hand in creating. Negotiate curfew hours or bedtimes, allowing them to pick within a range of reasonable times; ask them to choose among snack foods and television programs. Since they organize by telling themselves or others what they are going to do, have a weekly discussion about which chores are going to be done when.

Music tends to have a mood-changing effect on AKV children. Listening to music or stories or singing songs together can help them relax. Music they can do motions to or dance to is often a fun way for them to get moving or to use some of their energy creatively. The music they choose to listen to can also give you clues as to how they are feeling.

Provide frequent outlets for AKVs' physical energy. Encourage them to participate in sports of their choice; some will like team activities, others will prefer individual performance sports, like gymnastics or martial arts.

Invite them to walk when you want to discuss emotional subjects. Talking about feelings will make them want to move, and moving will help them access their feelings in a more steady way. Walk with them in a side-by-side fashion, so they can look wherever they are comfortable. Never insist on sustained eye contact. They cannot maintain it comfortably and can listen without it.

Touch will help AKV children settle down and get quiet. It is important to ask before touching. Let them choose how they want to make contact. Avoid telling them how they feel; instead, tell them what you notice about their body language or tone of voice and ask them how they feel.

Supporting Their Visual Channel

AKVs tend to be inventors, idea people. Encourage them to fully explore their visions and to do something with them; ask your AKV child to talk about his ideas in detail, what he imagines it would take to realize them, and what kind of help he might need.

Do not expect AKV kids to find something by simply pointing it out visually. Oral directions, like "It's close to the piano, near the window," will help them. If you write them a note or give them other visual input, make sure it is clear and simple.

AKVs may be especially timid about being seen or having pictures taken and very particular about how they look. Honor this sensitivity. Don't force them into photos. Understand that they may be shy when in public. Encourage them to discover the hairstyles and clothes that work for them.

Allow AKV children to have control over their eyes. Don't require them to maintain eye contact or to look at anything that may be painful or uncomfortable for them. Disturbing visual images may replay repeatedly in their minds for years. Teach them to be discriminating about what they watch. Once hooked on a television program, they can get "lost" and become deeply influenced. Invite them to talk about what they are seeing or reading. Their words can help them evaluate and make comfortable, aware choices.

Helping AKVs at Home

Children whose minds use the AKV pattern present what can be a confusing academic challenge for today's parents and teachers. They can easily learn and express what they know auditorily. Their verbal prowess creates an expectation of easy academic success. They are seriously challenged, however, by tasks which require their unconscious visual channel to focus in ways which are unnatural to it, most notably reading and writing. Until recently, there has been little flexibility in how these essential skills are taught, so children with the AKV thinking pattern are sometimes thought of as both "gifted" and "learning disabled." It is imperative that they be taught to read and write in ways suited to how their minds work.

As parents, you can most effectively support the development of your AKV children's reading and writing skills by working with the strengths of their learning pattern. They learn easily what they have heard and/or talked about. AKVs love to be read to; make this a regular practice, if possible. As their interest in reading builds, stop short of reading familiar lines or phrases and have them fill in the blank verbally. As they watch, they will begin to put together the word on the page with the sound they have spoken. Review words they recognize out loud with them frequently. Their desire to read and their personal experience will provide an important link between auditory and visual channels. Follow their excitement.

Once they've begun to read independently, AKVs may benefit from tracing the words on the page with their finger or reading aloud. Combining movement with reading may help these children stay alert. For example, sitting in a rocking chair or pedaling on a stationary bike may provide enough motion to keep them from spacing out while they are reading. Invite them to tell you or to act out what happens in the stories they read. Their ability to remember and evaluate what they've read (or seen) will come from their speaking about it.

AKV children may choose "easy" large print picture books or magazines for some time. Support them in selecting these books which are easier on their eyes. Their interest and comfort should be the most important considerations in book selection.

The physical task of writing can be difficult for some AKVs. Provide big paper and lots of space for younger ones to write big in learning their letters. Help them to remember how to form the letters with a rhyme like "A stick and circle makes a P, Add one on the bottom and it's a B." Personal meaning will also make this practice more enjoyable. Encourage them to write letters to friends and relatives, especially on cards where there are no lines. Invite them to write stories of their experiences. Have them dictate at first, with you as their scribe. Encourage them to do more and more of the writing themselves. Older children can use this method with a tape recorder for writing stories and papers. Train them early in the use of a typewriter or word processor. Understand that all written material, both what they create and what they receive, means a lot to people of this pattern. Verbally support them for every effort.

In general, schoolwork is very focused visually. Find out what they like to do to rest their eyes or what they look at to ease into a daydream. Help them become conscious of this physical need for balance. Discover together pleasurable ways to do this—watching clouds and sunsets, or walking in wide-open places.

AKVs memorize by saying material repeatedly. These kids are natural rap stars. Have them record, "lip sync," and create movements for what they must memorize. Put a rhythm or a song to spelling words, or make up a cheer. Encourage them to repeat the rhythm softly to themselves when they are writing their words. Have them bounce a ball or do familiar dance steps while they repeat what they must learn.

If you are trying to help these children learn a new skill, invite them to teach you what they already know and expand from there. They generally will learn best from a verbal explanation first and then a chance to do what they've just heard. Encourage them to speak each of the steps as they do it. When you think they have the concept, have them teach you how to do it. This may solidify the learning for them. Written instructions, diagrams, or examples can sometimes be confusing to AKVs. If you must use them, have your child read them out loud or explain what they see.

AKVs organize by telling themselves or someone else what they are going to do. These children will probably not be inclined to write down their assignments. If they become forgetful, have them tell you what they are going to do on a daily basis.

It may be helpful for AKV kids to study with the radio on.

They may be distracted by extraneous noise, a kind of auditory clutter, but they may concentrate better if they have music of their own choice in the environment.

◆ ◆ ◆

In summary, what these young leaders need most are an attentive ear, places to use their powerful energy, and encouragement to realize their many hopes and dreams.

6

The Verbal Gymnasts: AVK

"Treat people as if they were what they ought to be and you help them to become what they're capable of being."

—Goethe

Auditory-Visual-Kinesthetic

Easiest Way to Learn: Hear/See/Experience
Easiest Way to Express: Say/Show/Do

Pattern Snapshot

It's not hard to spot an AVK, because they can out-talk many adults. Indeed, AVK kids are often considered "smart" because they can easily verbalize what they think and keep up with the pace of adult conversations. Their words pour out in logical order all the time without hesitation. Their talk is largely conceptual, their vocabulary is relatively abstract; they love facts, history, and ideas of all kinds. They tend to be fascinated with languages and can often learn them easily. Music, storytelling, rhymes, humor, and puns are some of AVKs' delights. They enjoy explaining, debating, discussing, and arguing almost any idea. They are always trying to understand and want to help others do the same.

AVKs are usually voracious readers who are highly motivated in academics. However, hands-on activities, learning physical skills, or participating in sports may be frustrating and frightening for these kids. They are often shy about being touched and can have difficulty talking about feelings.

Language Characteristics

An AVK's world revolves around words. They usually begin talking at an early age. They rarely hesitate to talk to anyone, and love to discuss ideas, especially with people they think know more than they do—adults or older children. They frequently use auditory vocabulary, with words and phrases like "hear, say, sounds, understand," or "That rings a bell," "Let's play it by ear," and "Talk to you soon."

AVKs usually like to entertain others by telling jokes and funny stories, creating humorous poems, and making witty comments. They also love to try to make themselves invisible and eavesdrop on intriguing, adult conversations.

AVKs can be very demanding with their questions, especially "Why?" questions. They want so much to be listened to and to discover the answers. Teachers and parents often accuse them of talking too much, or not giving others a turn to speak. They can try to monopolize a conversation, interrupting others often. They tend to be selective listeners, paying attention only long enough to know if their question is being answered to their satisfaction.

AVK kids much prefer company to solitude; in fact it may be difficult for them to be alone. When they enter a room full of strangers, these children listen for the most interesting conversation to join.

They can memorize what they hear quite readily. Early "reading" for them is often actually memorizing books. They are usually very good students who ask intriguing questions and develop their own opinions easily. These children must talk in order to learn, and thus they learn best through discussion, where they can participate fully. AVKs respond to questions quickly and always have something to say, usually in a point by point fashion. They may get impatient with other students who don't have their verbal agility. They often prefer to learn independently where they can set the pace, and get individual attention from the teacher.

AVKs get expressive when they talk but their faces go flat when they move. They rarely use hand gestures when they speak; when they do, it will be for emphasis only.

Visual Characteristics

Most AVKs learn to read quite easily; a phonetic approach works well for them. They use books to feed their verbal knowledge and to continually add to their list of questions. They love to be read to and to read out loud.

These kids are typically good writers of both research and stories and proficient with spelling and editing skills. Their handwriting, however, is often hard to read.

Although AVKs can maintain steady eye contact, their eyes will blink, twitch, or flutter if they try to sustain it too long. They often need to look away to find their words, usually to the side.

Children with the AVK pattern have a middle visual channel that operates something like a zoom lens. They can see the whole of something and pay attention to the details of it at the same time. For example, they could be writing a term paper, working on developing each of the points they are making, and remain aware at the same time of the flow and intention of the paper as a whole. They can make visual images as well with their eyes open as closed. In their minds, they can see an issue from many perspectives.

They often experience confusion as many possibilities flashing simultaneously across the screen of their mind.

Physical Characteristics

AVK children may appear awkward or easily discouraged when first learning a physical activity. They may have great interest in hobbies or experiments they want to do with their hands and yet get very upset with their own clumsiness. Keeping a regular rhythm to music without visuals may be quite difficult. In order to learn movements or hand skills, they need words or metaphors that help them see what they have to do.

AVKs may not choose to compete physically in any way. It may be difficult for them to learn specific structured athletic skills, so they generally prefer free-form activities, such as running, dancing, skiing, or swimming. Given a choice, these kids often prefer reading to recess.

AVK children generally need a lot of variety in what they do. Because of this, their behavior may sometimes seem inconsistent. They find repetitive activity boring. To offset boredom, they may go from one activity to another and then back to the first, or create new approaches to a routine task rather than doing the same thing over and over.

Some AVK children have a hard time estimating the amount of time it takes to do something, especially new or lengthy tasks. It can also be difficult for them to know quickly what they want to do, so they may often start something and choose not to finish it.

AVKs typically have a very sketchy sense of their bodies. They tend to perceive their body as a whole, so pinpointing and naming specific sensations can be very difficult. They are capable of ignoring bodily signals for long periods of time.

About the only time AVK children are speechless is when they are asked about their feelings or body sensations. In their learning pattern, there is not a direct link between words and feelings (A - K); they need a visual link in between. They have to get silent and create an inner visual image to bridge these two channels and access this information. It may be very difficult for them to find words or they may take a long time in doing so. Many times, instead of telling you how they feel, they will articulately express the reasons for their feelings. However, these children tend to feel what they see on a deep level.

In general, AVKs may be very hesitant to talk about anything kinesthetic, particularly physical affection. A comfortable way for them to express affection is to say what they notice about you that they like. When angry, they typically yell or argue. AVKs may space out if you touch them, or ask them what they want to do, or how they feel. They tend to be quite shy about any kind of touch unless they know you quite well. They remember physical contact, both positive and negative, for a very long time. Poking, invasive touch can be difficult for them to cope with and can leave a harmful, lasting impression.

AVK Portrait

"Virginia seemed very studious, and in the first few weeks of fifth grade I mistook this for seriousness," Anne recalls. "She wore glasses and always had her nose in a book; she was the most curious person I have ever known. Her favorite book series was the World Book Encyclopedia; she once told me the best part was the `See Also' section at the end of each article—it led her mind in directions she might not have thought of on her own.

"My impression of studious Virginia changed dramatically on a November day when the kids gave oral book reports. Her passion was reading about famous women in history—Cleopatra, Harriet Tubman, Amelia Earhart, and this month's selection, Queen Elizabeth I. Virginia began with a straightforward summary of the monarch's life. But about half-way through her five minutes, she placed a crown on her head which transformed her ten-year-old body, face, and voice into `Liz' herself. (She told us to call her that!) Virginia's accent was perfect and she wove outrageously funny quips into her regal, historically-accurate monologue. The kids and I were in stitches and Virginia was obviously pleased with herself as she took her seat with a sly smile on her face. `Liz' was, indeed, a hard act to follow.

"At my invitation, on the last Friday of every month, right after lunch, Virginia brought to us another hysterical, historical person. Sometimes, our Friday visitor stepped off the pages of our social studies book; sometimes, she would surprise all of us. She and I worked together honing her research skills and helping her get a feel for each person's life and times. As Virginia's confidence in her learning increased, the monologues became dialogues; she courageously invited questions from the audience, which she insightfully answered in character. Even Virginia was amazed at how deeply she understood these famous figures. She brought all of herself to her learning and new vitality to our sense of history."

Communicating with AVK Children

Supporting Their Auditory Channel

What seems most important in talking with AVK kids is to assume that they understand what you are saying. Avoid talking down to them, and refrain from making the same point over and over. If you're not sure they have understood, ask them rather than repeat yourself. Use words that are as precise as possible. They can easily understand and enjoy subtleties of meaning. Realize that they grasp verbal instructions readily. If they seem confused, invite them to ask follow-up questions.

Set aside time to listen to your AVK kids; they appreciate it when they know you really are. Don't fake it. Tell them if you can't listen and resume the discussion when you can. Let them know you are listening by responding specifically to what they've said.

Encourage your AVK children to become more courteous listeners. Remind them not to interrupt. Tell them stories with surprise endings that will encourage them to listen all the way through. Encourage them to notice the sounds of the ocean and the trees, the purr of a cat, or their own heartbeat. Help them discover the communication that goes deeper than words.

Children with the AVK pattern are sensitive to how someone's words and voice tones affect them, but they may not be aware of the effect of *their* speaking on others. Repeating what they've said may help them to monitor what they say and how they say it.

Supporting Their Visual Channel

Share visual activities with your AVK children: read and discuss books and articles together, especially ones that express differing viewpoints, play card games with them, travel and discuss what you've seen.

Support AVK kids in using their visual channel to explore what may be challenging or confusing to them in their lives. Encourage them to write to themselves in a journal to allow their thinking to go deeper with the written word. Suggest that they write stories with different endings to help them discover which options feel right and make sense to them.

Help them discover how metaphor can add a new kind of meaning to their experiences. Does their life feel like a mountain climb? a treasure hunt? an ocean voyage? Encourage them to go back and forth like a zoom lens, examining important events in detail while heightening their perspective on how the events put together create a bigger picture of their life as a whole.

AVKs will need to look away to find their words; do not expect them to sustain eye contact for long periods of time.

Supporting Their Kinesthetic Channel

If your child is talking too fast or arguing relentlessly, suggest a kinesthetic or visual change to slow things down, help them go deeper, or alter the tone of the conversation. Invite them to go for a walk with you or sit next to them instead of in front of them. Encourage them to draw a picture or diagram or use color to illustrate what's going on.

Holding their hand or placing your hand on their shoulder will also shift their verbal activity. You can also change the pace of things with a different kind of question. Ask them how they are feeling. They will have to get quiet to access this information; using kinesthetic vocabulary—action and feeling words—will slow them down.

AVKs want respect and understanding for their need to do and learn physical things in their own, sometimes slow-paced and private way. Follow their lead in doing physical activities together. Allow them to set the pace and the length of a walk, a swim, or a bike ride.

Avoid using physical humor, such as tickling, pranks, or poking with AVK children. Stay with verbal humor, where these kids not only can hold their own, but shine.

When teaching them to do chores or other physical skills, talk to them, show them how you do it, and then invite them to develop their own way of doing it. Please don't insist that they do things exactly as you do. They may need privacy, space, and time to try things out on their own.

Helping AVKs at Home

Children with the AVK pattern usually have little trouble "succeeding" in school. Their verbal ability can take them far in the academic world. Unfortunately, this can make them especially impatient with the physical skills that they learn more slowly.

As parents, provide gentle encouragement for your AVK children to learn with their hands and bodies in their slower-paced way. Also, help them come to know the deeper satisfaction of taking their learning beyond concepts into real-life experiences.

AVK children never get all the verbal air time they need at school to solidify their learning. They always have questions and have an intrinsic need to say what they understand in their own words. Parents can support these children by setting aside time to listen, by having them tape record what they have to say and listening to it themselves, or by giving them opportunities to sing, be involved in plays, etc.

Seeing and experiencing what they are learning about can have a profound impact on AVK children. Make the learning come alive for them. If they're studying the fifty states, keep track of how many you visit or who you know who might live in each one. If they are interested in politics, take them with you to a community meeting, where they can witness or even get involved in local social action.

Help these kids develop their expertise by asking them their opinion on a wide range of topics, from the point of a television show to the reason they prefer vanilla to chocolate ice cream. Tell them what you are curious about, whether it's writing comedy, African drumming, or auto mechanics. Involve them in discussions about decisions which affect them.

Support any small way these children may want to be

physically active, but don't force them to play team sports. Allow them to make choices in this regard and encourage them to learn physical activities in small steps.

AVKs organize by talking about what needs to be done and jotting notes. Help them to keep track of their assignments by using this process.

Children with the AVK pattern memorize by saying material repeatedly. Putting facts into a rap song or rhyme may be fun and effective for AVKs. They may also do well recording and listening or "lip synching" to things they must memorize.

The level of quiet at home may be an important factor for AVK kids while studying. Some find extraneous noise very distracting and need to have complete quiet to concentrate; others can concentrate well with background music or outside sound.

Some AVK children have difficulty with planning in doing schoolwork, especially long-term projects. Teach them to break down long assignments into smaller tasks and to set realistic deadlines. Encourage them to plan variety into their timelines. They will get easily bored doing the same task for a long period of time and the quality will suffer.

In working on projects, AVKs can talk about what they want to do in elaborate detail, but they may try to plan something their hands cannot create easily. Encourage these kids to plan simple presentations.

◆ ◆ ◆

In summary, supporting AVKs means encouraging them to discover the ideas and questions that will broaden their perspective and helping them give voice to all that is inside of them.

7

The Movers and Groovers: KAV

"Creative thinking may simply mean the realization that there's no particular virtue in doing things the way they have always been done."
—Rudolph Flesch, educator

Kinesthetic-Auditory-Visual

Easiest Way to Learn: Experience/Hear/See
Easiest Way to Express: Do/Say/Show

Pattern Snapshot

You'll recognize KAV children by their strong, active bodies and their shy, sensitive eyes. They seem to be constantly in motion. Even when sitting, they are rarely still. Their preference is to relate to the world first in some tangible way—by touching, tasting, smelling, or experiencing anything new with their hands or their whole bodies. They tend to be well-coordinated, "natural" athletes who like competitive sports.

KAVs make eye contact in fleeting glances. Their handwriting is often immature and rarely neat. They are frequently reluctant readers and writers; they may take a long time to finish assignments that require these two skills, and often "daydream" or "space out" when asked to sit still and focus visually in class.

KAV kids are often affectionate, even cuddly. They love to touch and be touched. They usually enjoy talking about their feelings and their personal experiences.

Physical Characteristics

KAVs seem to have an endless supply of physical energy. In the classroom, they tend to be the fidgety ones, the foot jigglers, the gum chewers, the hair twirlers, the pencil biters, or those who make frequent trips to the bathroom or water fountain.

KAV kids learn things that involve the use of their bodies very easily. Their movements are strong, steady, direct, and detailed. They like to work with their hands: when they are younger, they frequently choose construction toys; older KAVs may tinker with cars, work with wood or crafts.

Children with the KAV pattern are competent "doers," preferring to be on their feet and in action rather than sitting at a desk. They generally have amazing physical stamina and do things in a logical fashion. They are frequent volunteers for errands and active classroom jobs.

Children with the KAV pattern are able to access and verbalize body sensations in a specific, organized way. They can tell you exactly where their head hurts or which muscle in their leg is pulled, or precisely where they want you to scratch their back. Physical comfort is quite important to KAVs. They may go to great lengths to find the right chair, the right position to sit in, or to choose the clothes that have just the right weight and texture.

Touch comes naturally and easily to most KAVs; it is a casual but important way to connect. They need both to touch and to be touched. In younger kids, if this need is not met in a positive way, they may resort to hitting or pushing in order to make some physical contact. Older KAVs may engage in early sexual activities if their need for touch has not been met in other non-sexual ways.

In general, these children are keenly aware of their emotions. But you won't see how they feel on their faces. KAVs generally have flat facial expressions; their bodies speak for them in how they stand, move, or touch. When they are angry, these kids tend to express it very physically with tantrums, throwing things, hitting, or acting out in other ways.

Language Characteristics

KAVs' hand gestures will often precede a spoken thought, as though the movement helps them conduct the words out, like a maestro's baton. These children enjoy talking about what they have been doing, how they did it, and how it felt to do it. They get bored easily with discussing abstract ideas. Very effective at talking about taking action, they use a lot of kinesthetic vocabulary—words and phrases that describe action or feeling, such as "getting a feel for," "How does that grab you?," or "I can't get a handle on it." They might end a conversation with "Catch you later," or "Let's get together soon."

KAVs are especially skilled at teaching people how to do things since translating action into words is easy for them. These children like to tell stories about experiences they've had; they frequently use kinesthetic metaphors when they speak. ("Throw it fast and fierce like a bullet.") They often want to convince others to do things their way.

Sometimes KAVs need to sort things out loud. They may start a conversation talking about the different choices they have, but by the end, they will know which option will work best for them as a result of having talked it through.

Visual Characteristics

Children with the KAV pattern are "eye-shy": maintaining

eye contact is very difficult for them. They prefer to keep their eyes averted, making occasional glances to check in with the person speaking. If required to "look" for too long, their eyes may seem distant or glazed over. They can listen intently, making little or no eye contact at all, even while busily doing something else. Many KAV children act timid or tough if they are being looked at, particularly by strangers in public. They also may be shy about having their picture taken.

KAVs are deeply influenced by the images that come in through their eyes. Nasty looks, ones that indicate judgment or criticism, can be more painful to these kids than even physical or verbal punishments. Smiles and looks of love and appreciation can likewise leave a lasting impression. Notes, cards, or pictures that are written or drawn for them can also affect KAVs for a long time. Older children of this pattern can be very choosy about the images they take in, particularly movies, TV programs, videos, and even room decorations.

KAVs are often reluctant readers; their eyes have difficulty focusing on tiny, closely-spaced print. Remembering sight vocabulary is difficult and they seem to get lost on the page. Thus, they tend to read infrequently, but when they do, they choose short, high-interest, large print picture books or magazines, which they get totally immersed in, remembering most easily what happened or how the characters felt in what they read.

Writing can be a laborious task for KAV children. They may have difficulty learning how to form the letters. Their writing style is often "immature" and rarely neat. These kids tend to be pile makers, sometimes needing to keep everything somewhat in sight rather than filed away in a drawer or desk. They can usually tell you easily in which pile what they are looking for is located.

Children with the KAV pattern can be easily overwhelmed

by visually detailed books, handouts, or room decorations, and so they tend to be "day-dreamers" at school. The prescription for them to space out is followed almost exactly in a lot of classrooms: sit still while being asked to listen and look at something specific. Often their "overly-active" bodies are trying to keep them alert and awake in a visually-demanding environment. They need visual input of all kinds to be simple and clear, and most of all, they need to move.

KAVs prefer to take in a wide view, the "bigger picture"; they can capture the whole of something with just a quick glance. Consequently, they are also expert "finders," able to locate a needle in an entire haystack.

Notes Anne, "I was out walking along the road to the beach one day when my young friend, Andrew, said to me, 'Isn't that the most beautiful one you've ever seen?' It took me quite a few minutes to find the gorgeous dragonfly he had spotted, well camouflaged in the reeds along the pond. His KAV eyes had found the treasure of that moment, out of the hundreds of things to look at near and far, a beautiful creature, paused in stillness."

KAV Portrait

"Scott was a bruiser of a kid for a fifth grader, hefty, a natural football player, a kid who seemed to approach every interaction with fists clenched and guard up," writes Anne about another of her former students. "The other kids mostly stayed out of his way, except in gym class where they picked him first for their teams. Scott's body spoke for him, poised for action, relaxing only with a touch or a tousle of his hair. I could watch him wind up in class, an emotional powder keg with a short fuse.

"His energy always felt too big for his place at the table of four. Reading or writing assignments meant fussing and fidgeting with lots of frustration; he'd tighten his jaw, clench his fists, and mutter under his breath."

"One day when this was happening, I pointed at the door to the playground and suggested that he take a lap or two to cool off. He came back and settled into his chair like he fit there. Much more self-contained, he got right to work. For several more days, as I sensed his concentration fall and his anger rise, I motioned toward the door and he bolted from his chair in great relief. And then came the day when, as I knelt beside another student, I felt Scott's presence next to me. I saw *his* hand motion toward the door, telling me that he knew what he needed and what he could do about it. That was a powerful moment, a moment of deep learning, when Scott read his own signals, trusted his own mind."

Communicating with KAV Children

Supporting Their Kinesthetic Channel

You can connect well with your KAV children by doing activities together, being physically affectionate, and letting them know you appreciate what they do and how well they do it. Plan family projects which include them: build a tree house, plant a garden, do spring cleaning, or cook a big company dinner. Ask them what regular family chores they would like to help with so they can experience how their efforts have really contributed. Have active fun together; play games and sports together.

Find out what they want to learn how to do. Invite them to teach you something they know and you don't. Exchange new ways of doing things. Recognize their physical expertise and help them expand it in ways they choose.

Don't insist that they sit still. Keep in mind that moving, wiggling, and fidgeting help them to stay alert. Provide opportunities where touch, taste, and smell can be a part of their first exposure to something new.

Understand the strong, healthy needs KAV children have for genuine touch. They respond well to a hug, a cuddle, a back rub. Cuddling with a stuffed animal or caring for a real pet are ways they can have contact when you are not around. Help them become aware of when they need physical contact. Encourage them to ask for what they need, so they won't resort to negative ways of getting this kind of attention.

If your child has tantrums or lashes out physically, set aside time when he or she is calm to talk about what happened, what all that energy felt like, and the message and needs that were hiding in the temper tantrum. Consider the tantrum as a communication that he or she didn't know how to fit into words, rather than simply reacting to it or ignoring it. Set up, in advance, some kind of physical activity, such as going outside and throwing rocks, which can be done when frustrated, until words shape themselves from all of that energy.

Respect your KAV children's need to be physically comfortable. They will be easily distracted by clothes that don't fit well or that irritate their skin. Understand that they may have to adjust their position continually to maintain comfort. They may be very particular about bedding, furniture, and the feel of their sports equipment. It is rumored that the princess who felt a pea under her mattress was a KAV!

Supporting Their Auditory Channel

Invite KAV kids to talk about their feelings and their personal experience. Instead of asking, "What are you thinking?", try "What are you feeling?" or "What have you been doing?"

Verbal communication with KAVs will be most effective if it includes a kinesthetic component. Talk while doing something: walking, playing basketball, or cooking dinner. Having something to hold and play with in their hands may also help KAVs pay attention. Sometimes, KAV kids will want to be physically close in conversation. If this is the case, sit or stand side-by-side to allow them to speak more easily without prolonged eye contact.

As much as possible, speak to KAV children in action or feeling words; explain things in terms of how to do something, how it works, or how it might feel. Allow time for them to sort things out loud when they are confused. It's important for them to talk through and evaluate what they hear and to learn to speak what's true for them.

Music can have a powerful effect on the emotional and physical state of KAV children. Soothing songs or instrumental music may be effective in helping them settle down or ease into sleep. They can also find singing and playing music satisfying— as an outlet for both their creative self-expression and their physical energy.

Supporting Their Visual Channel

KAVs have minds that can see the whole of a situation in a glance and observe solutions from a wide perspective; at the same time, they find it difficult to notice visual details. For example, they can look at someone and tell you what that person is feeling without noticing the color of his or her eyes or what he or she is wearing.

Ask KAV children about their dreams, and their imaginings. Talk with them about a step-by-step action plan which will make it possible to convert a vision or picture into reality.

Respect the sensitivity of their visual channel. Please don't tell them what to look at or what they did or did not see. Encourage them to trust their own eyes and to notice how they are affected by what they take in visually. Honor their decisions to hide their eyes or move away from visual images that may be painful or uncomfortable for them. Both pleasant and unpleasant "pictures" can stay in their minds for a long time.

Teach them to make careful choices about what they watch. Once KAVs get involved visually in a television program, movie, photograph, or work of art, they can become totally lost in it and deeply influenced by it. Talking with them about what they are seeing or reading can help them make comfortable choices.

Helping KAVs at Home

Some children with the KAV pattern have a very difficult time in school. Their abundant physical energy is sometimes labeled "hyperactivity." When they "space out" in class, often triggered by the visual input of most learning environments, they are said to have an "attention deficit." When their eyes respond to the strain of having to focus consistently on tiny print, they are called "dyslexic."

These labels represent well-meaning attempts by educators to figure out why some of these children are not responding to traditional classroom instruction. Perhaps, an understanding of the KAV learning pattern will help parents and teachers come closer to meeting the educational needs of these children. Even for those who have not been so labeled, the visual demands and physical restrictions of traditional classrooms can make their schooling experience a frustrating one. Parents of KAV children can support them effectively by providing what is only minimally offered at most schools—opportunities to use their bodies to learn and their eyes to create.

KAV children remember most easily what they've handled or experienced. Supplement reading and writing assignments with chances to get physically involved with whatever they're studying. Let them attach wires from batteries to test bulbs and complete a circuit themselves so they can help a demonstration or book diagram come alive. Take field trips together. If your

KAV child is learning about old sailing ships, for example, visit the Constitution, providing opportunities to walk on the deck, turn the wheel, and lay down in the crewman's hammock. After such an experience, the stories of the ship's history, or pictures and diagrams will have personal meaning.

Making models of the water cycle or the Battle of Bunker Hill will reinforce class discussions and textbook chapters. Acting out the stories in your KAV's reading book or the word problems in math will increase his or her comprehension and skill development.

Encourage your KAV child to play outside or participate in sports before doing homework. This will help balance out the sedentary nature of the typical school day and will make concentration easier when the time comes to sit down and work.

Find ways to ease the pressure and the difficulty of the reading and writing process on your KAV children while at home. It may be difficult for them to read without spacing out, if they are not rocking, jiggling, or moving. Sitting in a rocking chair or pedaling a stationary bike may provide enough movement to keep them from daydreaming while they are reading. Following along with their fingers on the page of print may help, too. Reading out loud sometimes helps them maintain concentration.

Invite your KAV children to tell you about what happens in the stories they read. Ask them questions to help them discover how their feelings and experiences may be similar to the characters they are reading about. This will reinforce their comprehension. They may be most comfortable choosing large print picture books or magazines for some time.

The eye-to-hand coordination required by writing can be difficult for some younger KAVs. Get an easel, a chalkboard, or tape large paper to the wall so they can practice with their whole bodies and write big while they are learning to write their letters. Understand that their way of writing may never be neat and standardized.

The content of KAVs' writing should first come out of their experience. Encourage them to write stories of times they remember, or to send letters to friends about what they are doing. At first, be their secretary, writing down the words for them so they can have the pleasure of creating without the struggle of trying to visually remember the details of English.

Encourage your KAV children to find ways to express their dreams and inner images. Help them explore the more creative aspects of their visual channel to balance the more focused aspects emphasized in school. Suggest dabbling at home with different kinds of art supplies, such as paints, clay, pastels, craft materials, or wood.

After being asked to concentrate in a visually-detailed way for much of the school day, KAV children will probably need opportunities to "space out" and take in the world more "widely." Help them discover what visual images are soothing and pleasant to look at. Invite them to take a walk with you and watch the clouds together, for example.

KAVs are very aware of their environment. Help them create study places where they can both move around and be comfortable while sitting. Discover together what works well with regard to furniture, light, warmth, fresh air, and moisture in the environment.

◆ ◆ ◆

In summary, these moving and grooving kids need to be given fun and practical outlets for their overflowing physical energy, as well as loving touch and attention while they tell you of their feelings, hopes, and dreams.

8

The Wandering Wonderers: KVA

"Comparing East Asian and American elementary schools, we found little difference in the percentages of students with reading disabilities. What differed remarkably was parents' attitudes—the American parents tended to focus on innate disabilities, the Asians on the students' efforts."
—Harold Stevenson and James Stigler

Kinesthetic-Visual-Auditory

Easiest Way to Learn: Experience/See/Hear
Easiest Way to Express: Do/Show/Say

Pattern Snapshot

KVA kids are those private, quiet nature lovers who have a strong physical presence and seem to be surrounded by a deep silence. They have smooth, receptive energy and are generally graceful in their bodies. They seem to come alive when they are moving. Naturally well-coordinated, these children can learn physical tasks easily without verbal instruction.

KVAs are usually soft-spoken kids who always seem to be sensing and watching the actions of others. Words come slowly and concisely. It may be especially difficult for them to talk about feelings. They can become overwhelmed easily by having to listen to too many words. These kids are fairly private people who enjoy working or playing alone or with one special friend. It is often easier for them to relate to animals than to people.

KVAs often are interested in seemingly diverse and dissimilar things. These are the kids who love both football and art, sewing and chemistry. They seem to have an intuitive sense of how it all fits together.

Physical Characteristics

Movement is very important to KVA children. They have a lot of physical energy. They can be wiggly if asked to sit still; some seem to be constantly in motion. They will be most attentive if given the choice to stand and stretch or keep their hands busy while watching and listening.

KVAs like to be "doing" as much as possible; they love to participate in sports and can learn new physical skills with ease. Physical activity of any kind tends to bring them more fully alert. These children can be very well organized and detailed in what they do. They are diligent workers when they believe that they can succeed. They generally have good eye-hand coordination, often like working with their hands, and are easily able to put things together, sometimes in very creative ways.

KVA children are generally very aware of the specific sensations in their bodies. Since physical comfort is quite important to them, they may go to great lengths to find the right chair or the right position to sit in. They tend to choose clothes that are comfortable and allow freedom of movement, with some awareness of how they look.

KVAs feel things deeply, but it may be almost impossible for them to express their emotions in words. They can become sullen and stubborn if they feel someone important to them is not on their side. When they are angry they tend to withdraw rather than lash out. Touch comes naturally and easily to KVAs, and they need both to touch and to be touched.

Children with the KVA pattern tend to choose to be alone or with one or two others rather than be a part of a large social gathering. If they are in a group, they will often look for a quiet place to sit back, watch, and listen.

Visual Characteristics

KVA children can maintain steady eye contact, but their eyes blink, twitch, or flutter if they try to sustain it too long. Their eyes will glaze over if they listen to too many words, and they usually need to look away to the side to find what they want to say.

Children with the KVA pattern have a three-dimensional way of making images. This means that literally and figuratively they see things from many perspectives. They can turn letters, words, pictures, designs, and diagrams around in their minds. They can also see the validity of many sides of an issue and the whole of something as well its details.

Many KVA children have trouble learning to read if they are taught with a typical phonics approach, since sounding out words can be ineffective with them. Even if they are able to decipher a word one time, they may not be able to remember it later. In slowing down to figure out a strange word, KVAs easily lose the context of the story. They may need to use a finger to keep track of their place on the page.

Language Characteristics

KVA children need to feel safe, accepted, and listened to in order to converse. They are often very quiet and self-conscious about speaking in groups. They don't like to talk off the top of their heads, and may freeze if pressured to speak.

Even when they feel comfortable, words often don't come easily for KVAs. There may be pauses in their speech. They frequently take a long time to answer a question, find the name of something, or the word they're looking for. Their answers may be short, concise, and sometimes surprisingly unique and insightful. Their responses may be circular, sometimes never getting to the point, and they seem to ask endless questions that often cannot be answered.

KVA children frequently use a lot of kinesthetic vocabulary, words that convey action or feelings, like "grab, hold, soft," or "move," and phrases like "That feels right," or "I'll be in touch soon." They rarely chit-chat, and often forget titles or what initials stand for. Their facial expressions usually go flat when they speak.

Some KVA children may be slow to begin speaking in early childhood; they may be the ones who surprise their parents by being completely silent until they suddenly speak in full sentences. They sometimes have their own unique pronunciations for words that they continue to use for a long time.

KVA children may get overwhelmed easily by a lot of words and space out if they have to sit still, look intently at something, and listen, because the unconscious part of their mind is being triggered. This also means that they are affected deeply by what is said to them. Harsh or critical phrases can echo in their minds for years. Whenever possible, criticism should be written, not spoken.

KVA Portrait

"Steve was a child I would describe as sweet, in that rich,

dark chocolate kind of way," Anne remembers. "He had smooth, easy energy and his body was toned like a strong, young thoroughbred's. He was a very private kid, quiet, steady in his work habits, but one who never had the pleasure of much success in the classroom.

"In the first week of fifth grade, we made collage-like portraits to introduce ourselves; in the center of Steve's was a photo of himself holding a soccer ball. Around the outside, in meticulous print, he wrote the names of all the sports he loved, everything from skateboards and dirt bikes to swimming and ice hockey, each carefully illustrated with little cartoon-like characters he loved to draw.

"That year, for the last half hour of every day, we had what was called Magic Circle. This was a chance for the kids to share with each other their feelings about various topics in a very safe setting. No one could interrupt and everyone had the right to pass. For the first few months, Steve fidgeted a lot, but never spoke; he would always pass, choosing simply to listen to his classmates, many of whom were jumping at the chance to talk about their feelings. He seemed a little embarrassed, but thirty minutes was never quite long enough for him to muster his courage, or find his words.

"One day, something clicked for Steve. The topic for the day was something about sports, a time when we had helped a team win, I think. Much to everyone's surprise (and my delight), Steve talked about a soccer game in which he had scored the winning goal. `I felt proud,' he said.

"The next day, he brought in a picture of a funny little dog drawn on manila tagboard. It was very cleverly designed—holes were cut out and there were strips attached to the back which let the eyes move back and forth. Underneath `Charlie' was the label `Proud.' A new Charlie would appear every few days, each one with a new body posture and eyes conveying a different emotion. He brought the Charlies to Circle with him every day. Sometimes looking at his Charlies would help him find the words to describe how he was feeling. Sometimes he would simply hold up a picture and let Charlie do the talking for him. After that, Steve rarely passed, having found a fun, creative way to share his feelings and experiences that also respected the slow pace of his words."

Communicating with KVA Children

Supporting Their Kinesthetic Channel

KVAs want to be joined in activity, to be touched, and to be appreciated for what they know how to do. The most effective connections with KVA children begin with doing something together. Play games with them, following their lead. Practice and play sports together. As much as possible, be out in nature with them. Find ways to share active projects: build a go-cart, do chemistry experiments, make cookies, plant trees. Involve them in family chores where they can experience how their efforts have really contributed: wash the dog, rake the leaves, vacuum the carpet, paint a room. Ask what they want to learn how to do. Invite them to teach you something they know and you don't. Exchange new ways of doing things.

Allow them to be up and moving, or using their hands even if you want to sit still. Provide opportunities where touch, taste, and smell can be a part of their first exposure to something new.

Understand the strong, healthy needs KVA children have for genuine touch: a hug, a cuddle, a back rub. They typically love to care for animals. Having a pet of their own can help them satisfy their needs to touch and communicate in non-verbal ways.

If your KVA child tends to withdraw when his or her feelings are hurt, give some space. Don't verbally prod. A gentle touch may be the best way to help reconnect when he or she is ready.

Supporting Their Visual Channel

It is very effective to use the visual channel to communicate with KVAs so they can have a breather from talking and listening: write them notes.

Have fun with their ability to move images around. They can be great Boggle or Scrabble or MasterMind players for just this reason.

Encourage any budding interest they may have in the arts, photography, drawing, sculpture, weaving, woodworking. This may give them a nonverbal way of expressing how they feel.

Find activities that involve looking at something together: pictures they've drawn, a favorite TV program, a sporting event, a movie, card games.

Supporting Their Auditory Channel

Above all, have patience with KVAs' silence and their need for it. Allow them to come to you with questions and statements. Prodding them to talk can make them retreat further into themselves.

Avoid chit-chat or small talk with your KVA children. Invite them to tell you about their experiences—they will talk more comfortably about what they've done than about how they feel. If you ask them a question, allow them some silent time to think. Don't tell them what they think or finish their sentences. Listen all the way through, even if you think you know what they are going to say. They may surprise you.

KVAs navigate through their lives by asking endless questions, looking for possibilities, and living out the answers. No matter how much you are tempted, do not answer these questions. Bring their attention back to themselves. Sometimes just being silent is the best way to do that—or answer with an honest "I don't know."

Encourage KVA kids to move or draw or play with something while conversing, and let them look where they want to. Provide actual or mental pictures or concrete examples when explaining a new or abstract concept.

Be truthful and literal when speaking with them. Don't exaggerate unless you make it clear that you are. Be aware that they are very sensitive to negative tone of voice as well as words. What you say to them, and how you say it, will go in deeply.

Listening to KVAs' favorite music with them can be a powerful and intimate way to connect.

Helping KVAs at Home

Typically, KVA children are most enthusiastic about the parts of school that allow them to express their physical energy and coordination—physical education, art, woodshop, and lab sciences. The traditional visual and auditory ways of learning do not fully satisfy the educational needs of most KVAs; school often leaves them either lulled and withdrawn, or ready to explode with unreleased energy. These children want to be actively engaged and involved in everything; they want to do, they want to know how, they want to be skillful. They also need quiet to integrate information fully. School lets them down on both counts. Their natural capabilities are misunderstood and largely untapped.

As a parent, you can most effectively support your KVA children by offering them both physical activities and silent solitude. Directing their physical energy into a sport or other activity in the hours after school will increase their ability to concentrate on homework assignments later.

When these children arrive home from school, understand

that they may need a lot of quiet time to balance out the typical, highly verbal school day. Provide opportunities for them to be out in nature or in their own rooms where they can choose silence or their own music.

Whenever possible, provide opportunities for KVA children to experience what they are learning about; field trips and hands-on experiences are often their best teachers. If they are learning about the space program, take them to the space museum so they can climb into an actual capsule and sit behind the control panel, or find a video that will give them that feeling.

When helping your KVA child study, as often as possible, follow the pattern of "experience, see, hear" and "do, show, say." To study spelling words, for example, trace their words on their backs so they can feel them. In the process, they can see the word in their mind's eye before you tell them. Then, have them write and say the word themselves to complete the loop.

Children with the KVA pattern should be taught to read and write with a "whole language experiential approach." Provide as many pieces of this for them at home as possible if they aren't being taught that way in school: Encourage them to tell you stories from experiences they've had that they want to remember. Their motivation will be much higher if it is their own words they are reading and writing. Write for them.

Encourage KVA kids to be in motion while reading. Stationary bikes or rocking chairs may provide just enough motion so they can concentrate. Encourage them to imagine themselves taking part in the stories or actually invite them to act them out. Illustrating the story or taking notes may help them remember what they've read. When they must give oral presentations, encourage your KVA children to use notes, props they can hold, or to move around. Reviewing concepts for a test or studying spelling can often be easier with visual games or flashcards. A wall-mounted chalkboard or easel may be a useful, fun study tool: review math concepts by doing problems on the board. Their bodies will be up and active while they work.

Most KVA children are well aware that they space out when people are talking. Experiment with them to find the best non-distracting ways for them to move their bodies or hands to stay alert while listening.

Help them create a study place for themselves where they can both move around and be comfortable while sitting. Support them in making the space fit their needs for warmth, fresh air, and moisture.

◆ ◆ ◆

In summary, these wandering, wondering children need to be given opportunities to actively explore their many interests, encouragement to find creative ways to express how they feel, and comfortable silence that will help them find their own voice.

9

The Seer/Feelers: VKA

"If an unfriendly foreign power had at-
tempted to impose on America the medi-
ocre educational performance that exists
today, we might well have viewed it as an
act of war."
—The National Commission On
Excellence in Education

Visual-Kinesthetic-Auditory

Easiest Way to Learn: See/Experience/Hear
Easiest Way to Express: Show/Do/Say

Pattern Snapshot

You may be struck right away by the empathetic energy of VKA children. They seem to drink in the world through their eyes and feel what they see. At times, especially in large groups, they can be rather quiet and to themselves. At other times, they can be very talkative, telling lengthy personal stories which can be quite difficult to follow. Their words may go around in circles and never seem to get to the point. VKAs must use their hands or move around in order to speak.

They sometimes have a difficult time making decisions for themselves; VKAs can be easily swayed by the crowd. When things don't turn out as they expect, they can resort to whining.

VKAs have excellent eye-hand coordination; they can easily learn to do something by watching someone else and then trying it themselves. They are good collaborators, partners, and co-workers, preferring to work in groups or on teams rather than independently.

Visual Characteristics

These children are visually meticulous; they often want their clothes, possessions, and surroundings to fit an inner image they are trying to create. They can't think well with visual clutter. Most of them have legible handwriting, good spelling, and proofreading ability. Many like to draw and design things in detail. They tend to depend on written reminders, lists, instructions, and directions to keep themselves well organized.

VKAs connect with others most easily by making eye contact. They can often maintain it steadily, but their eyes glaze over if they are listening too long. They also tend to look up frequently when thinking and may have to close their eyes to listen in depth.

VKAs remember most easily what they have seen or read. They will recall people's faces, but often not their names. They learn best by watching a demonstration or reading the directions for a task and then doing it, *without being told first how to do it*. If they get stuck in the process, then they might ask questions and want some explanation. If you were teaching a young VKA to tie her shoes, for example, it would be best to show her first without even describing your actions. Then, let her do it herself as much as she wants, going back and forth between showing and doing. Only if she asks a question should you offer any words in the process, since they might cause confusion.

It is also important for VKAs to know that they can practice and make mistakes while learning without being criticized. Harsh or ridiculing words can put a stop to their learning process altogether.

Some VKAs are voracious readers, while others have lifelong difficulty with reading, depending on how they are taught. For VKAs, the visual and auditory channels—the two modes involved in reading—are separated by the middle kinesthetic channel. So, unless a VKA's body, hands, feelings, or experiences are engaged in the process somehow, reading can be difficult. A phonics approach is rarely effective since it is hard for VKAs to sound out words or to remember them when they do. A sight decoding process, where the student uses flashcards and learns the look and shape of words, works much better. It usually helps for young VKAs to follow along with their fingers while reading. Oral reading can be extremely difficult and anxiety-producing for them.

These children usually like to take copious notes. It is easy for them to write almost word for word what they hear. They memorize most easily by writing something repeatedly, so you may find them recopying their notes from class.

Physical Characteristics

VKAs often have excellent eye-hand coordination. They can excel at video games; they love to take things apart, and are often keenly interested in how things work, everything from complex machines to the human body.

Physical activity tends to be an important emotional and energetic outlet for VKAs. They usually have a lot of wound-up physical energy just below the surface. They are often good athletes, who learn physical tasks easily when shown.

VKA children can be somewhat hesitant about physical contact. They need to make eye contact before being touched.

Children with the VKA pattern frequently are aware of the sensations in their bodies. Likewise, their feelings are often easily accessible to them. VKAs can also pick up the feelings and sensations being experienced by others they see around them.

It can be quite difficult for VKAs to learn how to cope with all of what they feel and sense inside. They need to find effective ways for expressing and releasing their emotions. If this doesn't happen, they can become quite anxious and resentful. They have a tendency to hold grudges for a long time if they don't know how to clear their emotions. When they are angry, these children express it with dirty looks, gestures, or by sending nasty notes.

The expressions of these kids seem to come alive when they move, but their faces go flat when they speak. They must move their hands or their bodies as they talk, since the motion is helping the words find their way out.

Most VKAs prefer to join with others in collaboration rather than work or play by themselves. They are great partners and helpers, though they may hesitate to take a leadership role. Some of them can get very involved in the social life of their peer group, especially in the gossipy emotional details of everyone's relationships.

VKA children often have a tough time making decisions, as they often feel pulled in two directions and vacillate a lot before making up their minds. They may simply follow the crowd rather than take the time needed to come to a clear choice for themselves. Experience seems to be their best teacher in sorting things out. If they can see and try out their options, they can often know what's right for them. If a decision is made for them, they will not feel satisfied and may resort to complaining.

Language Characteristics

In large discussion or lecture groups, VKA kids tend to be quiet and keep to themselves. It is difficult for them to speak off the top of their heads. There may be long pauses between their words or phrases when they speak, and they can get confused and space out when required to listen for long periods or when asked questions about what they have heard.

With one or two peers, however, VKAs can be very talkative. Adults may have trouble following their conversation since they may spiral with their words, a tendency we call pinwheeling; they jump from topic to topic repeatedly, making connections in their speaking which may not be understandable to the listener, and which may never seem to get to the point.

Children with the VKA pattern use lots of visual vocabulary—words that paint images and phrases that include "look, see, show, imagine," "I can picture that," or "See you soon." They tend to ask endless questions that have no answers. If you attempt to answer them, frequently their response begins with "Yeah, but . . . . "

VKAs remember for a long time what they have been told about themselves, whether positive or negative, and they may feel invaded by a harsh tone of voice or verbal criticism.

VKA Portrait

Anne remembers, "Tiffany was truly a live wire. Her lithe young body, crowned with red curly hair and electric blue eyes, literally flitted around any room she was in. She loved to have lunch with me; we had a regular date, every Thursday at 12:15. For a solid half hour, between bites, she would weave a verbal tapestry, telling me in non-stop detail about everything going on in her life: from the lace her mother was sewing on her new dress, to the jewelry she had seen in the store window, to her brother's pet gerbil, to her favorite aunt who was coming to visit, to her upcoming soccer practice. All the while, her blue eyes sparkled, and her hands never stopped moving.

"Tiffany loved to talk and found that few people in her life had the patience to listen to her hard-to-follow ribbons of words that never seemed to go anywhere. I was fascinated with how she thought and was somewhat concerned about her as a student. She had a hard time paying attention in class. In calling on her, I could almost count on her not knowing what the question was. When we were doing seatwork, I would watch her; she followed every stray sound in the room, endlessly distractable. I was at a loss as to how to help her.

"I asked her how she felt in reading class. She said she wanted to look at everything in the room *but* the page in front of her. She couldn't concentrate enough on the words to understand the stories; it never got quiet enough and every word that she read seemed to echo in her head.

"One Thursday, as Tiffany brought her tray into the classroom, I was pawing through a box of buttons on the counter, getting ready for the afternoon art project. She joined me at the counter and was totally taken in by one big, velvet-covered button in the box. I asked if she would like to have that one to keep and her blue eyes lit up as she said,`Oh, yes!'I told her that this was a special button, one that might actually help her concentrate better in class.`Sometimes holding something that beautiful in your hand can help you hold your attention while you read.'

"At first, she had a puzzled look on her face. As she rubbed the maroon softness with her thumb, I said `That's right, just like that. Let's try it for a week and see what happens.'

"Something as simple as a button helped Tiffany's hands link her eyes and ears in the reading process. As her self-confidence grew, we moved from the button, to rubbing her arm, to simply taking a breath."

Communicating with VKA Children

Supporting Their Visual Channel

Writing may be a more effective way of communicating with VKAs than speaking. They will be able to grasp more easily what you are trying to convey than if you say it to them. Encourage them to write as well. This will allow their thoughts to come into focus and help them communicate more succinctly with less spiraling.

Reading what they have written will help them find the cohesive meaning in what they are thinking. Their thoughts can sometimes feel like fractured phrases to them. Writing is also an effective way for them to express the many feelings they have inside.

In conversations with VKAs, give them as much eye contact as possible. Write down what they say for them so they can refer to it later. Otherwise what they have said may seem to evaporate in their mind. Encourage them to take notes during phone conversations or in any other important verbal communication. Also, write down the questions they are currently wondering about. This will help them think for themselves as they live out the answers.

VKAs will know that you care for them most clearly from letters, notes, cards, or other visual remembrances, such as gifts or flowers.

Supporting Their Kinesthetic Channel

In being so aware of how others feel, VKAs can easily lose their sense of themselves. Because of this, it is essential for them to learn to recognize their own body signals and emotions as distinct from everyone else's. Otherwise, in order to protect themselves from feeling too much from others, they may learn to shut down their awareness of sensation altogether and not be in touch with their own bodies.

Encourage your VKA children to take the time to discover how they feel. Frequently turn their attention to themselves with questions like: What are you feeling right now? What is this like for you? Suggest they move or take physical space in order to find their answers.

Rhythm is kinesthetic. Help VKAs find their own, by teaching them to clap or tap a beat that feels like their energy. Once they find their rhythm, it may be easier for them to find their own words.

Encourage your VKA children to find out what they want, not what they think they should want. Suggest that they talk with themselves in the mirror to discover this. When they are looking only at themselves, they can feel their own feelings better than when they are around other people. Solitude will help them when they feel pulled in two directions at the same time.

If not taught and encouraged to find their own unique style, these kids can feel like they are living everyone else's life. It is easy for them to claim others' behaviors as their own. If they don't know themselves and their own values, they may be too willing to go along with the crowd.

Supporting Their Auditory Channel

VKAs are easily influenced by what they are told about themselves. Make sure that your words and tone of voice support their positive self-esteem. What you say to them will go in very deeply. Whenever possible, criticism should be written, not spoken.

Avoid using sarcasm with VKAs. Their auditory channel is very literal. They will take in the biting tone of voice and may not understand at all what you say.

It is vital for these children to feel heard. Allow them time to speak; have patience with their spiraling words. Really listen and mirror back to them in words or in writing what they have said. Let them know that what they think counts with you.

VKAs need to ask a lot of questions. Don't answer them. Instead, direct their attention back to themselves--their own words, experiences, or viewpoints. Allow time for silence and for pauses in the midst of conversations--do not finish the sentences of VKAs, interrupt them, or put words in their mouths.

It is often more effective to ask them, "How do you feel about . . . ?" rather than "What do you think about . . . ?" It will help them stay more present to focus on feelings. Asking their opinion can cause them to space out. Pay attention to when VKAs eyes glaze over. You may be talking too fast, too intensely, or too abstractly. When they get stuck trying to express some-thing, invite these children to show you what they want to say with their hands.

Helping VKAs at Home

School can be a "mixed bag" for children with the VKA pattern. They are often very good readers who have a difficult time accessing and articulating what they have learned. They can be very competent, even creative, writers. Unfortunately, the educational emphasis on lecturing and listening diminishes their confidence in their ability to learn.

As parents, you can most effectively support your VKA children's self-esteem by respecting their auditory sensitivity, and helping build on visual strengths. When VKA children arrive home from school, understand that some of them may need a lot of quiet time to balance out the typical, highly verbal school day. Others may need to be listened to. Home may be the only place they feel comfortable speaking. They may need to put together the learnings of their day out loud. Be patient with their pauses and the circular pattern of their words. Take notes for them so they will have a visual model of what they have said. Encourage them to add to your notes later.

Support the reading skills of your VKA kids. They have good visual memories for words. Use flashcards to help them learn the looks of unfamiliar words. Point out visual similarities among word families that will help them learn whole groups of words at once. Encourage these children to make pictures in their minds of the stories they read. This is a natural skill for them, one that will help them with comprehension and retention. Otherwise some will get stuck in the process of sounding out the words. Encourage VKAs to follow along in the book with their finger. Try giving them a snack while reading; for some this will keep them from spacing out.

Make reading a family activity. Children of this pattern love to be read to. Go to the library together. Help your younger VKAs build their skills on books that match their most avid interests.

Provide a special public place to display your VKAs interests and accomplishments. These children can be very creative with their hands, so include art projects, scientific inventions, and decorations as well as photos of special places and events, trophies, certificates, special notes, cards, or letters they've received. Having a place where these important things can be seen may mean more to your child than verbal congratulations.

VKAs remember best what they have seen or experienced. Relating new concepts to something they have lived through, or finding a visual image will really help them grasp things. Find ways to help them do something with what they are learning. Make math concepts obviously useful with practical applications, such as building, cooking, or gardening. Find many opportunities for them to be with people who are using what they are learning so they can watch. Visit scientists, craftspeople, chefs, mechanics, and computer operators, for example.

Avoid long verbal explanations when helping these children. They respond best to being shown how to do something and then being given the space to try it themselves. When the use of words is all that is available, relate what they are learning to an experience they have had, use visual images, or touch them.

Oral presentations can be among the most anxiety-producing experiences for VKAs in school. Encourage them to prepare written notes to help focus what they will say. The use of props that they can talk about will also help them trust that they can remember their words. Listen while they practice and give them feedback about what they do well. Help them find lively images and experiences they can bring to mind and talk from, especially if they get stuck.

VKAs may not be able to think with visual clutter. Help them set up a study area that they can keep relatively neat, with just enough color or things to look at without being distracting.

◆ ◆ ◆

VKA children thrive on seeing and feeling love from the little things you do for them, your frequent touches, and little notes of encouragement which focus on what they have done well.

10

The Show and Tellers: VAK

*"The real teacher, in fact, lets nothing else
be learned than—learning."*
—Martin Heidegger

Visual-Auditory-Kinesthetic

Easiest Way to Learn: See/Hear/Experience
Easiest Way to Express: Show/Say/Do

Pattern Snapshot

VAKs are the children with the bright and shiny eyes who could have invented "Show and Tell." They love to read and point out everything they've seen. Many VAKs make a visual impression with the clothes they wear, which are usually chosen in colorful, well-coordinated outfits designed to look good. These children are list makers with neat legible handwriting. They are generally good students.

VAKs are people who love to tell stories and are often persuasive in their speaking. They're natural teachers and may try to convince you of almost anything. They have lots of feeling behind their words and you can usually see how they feel from the look on their faces.

These kids have a sketchy sense of their bodies and may have to do a physical action over and over in order to learn it. They tend to shy away from competitive sports. VAKs can be very private about their feelings; touch is not casual for them, so they are often hesitant to make physical contact.

Visual Characteristics

VAK children are open, eager, and curious. Their eyes light up their faces, and they can maintain eye contact easily throughout most conversations. They enjoy looking at and creating visual detail. They love just to *look* at possibilities, to flip through catalogs, to go windowshopping, or to people-watch.

Young VAKs may like to color in coloring books; many prefer the precision of this to painting and drawing. They can also be great doodlers. They enjoy board games, card games, puzzles, and word play.

VAK children love to have everything neat and orderly, but they may get bored with keeping their own things that way. They enjoy visually organizing other people's things and doing tasks like grading papers. They often volunteer to be teachers' or parents' helpers.

These children have no trouble remembering what they have seen or read. They learn well from demonstrations or from reading on their own, from handouts, charts, or diagrams as learning tools.

VAKs generally like to take notes, though they may not need to go back to them until right before a test, if at all. They are usually good test-takers who memorize by reading, writing, and saying out loud what they need to learn. They can keep lots of details stored visually, sometimes to the point of having a photographic memory.

VAK children can be real show-offs and performers who

play to any audience. Some can also be overly helpful at times, wanting to make and maintain a good impression on the adults in their lives.

Most VAKs are avid readers; they seem to devour as much as possible of anything in print. A typical phonics approach usually works well for them. Reading is generally the easiest way for them to learn something. They are also good at spelling, editing, and proofreading, and their writing tends to be clear and well-organized, with neat, legible penmanship.

Children with the VAK pattern are the kids whose feelings are written all over their faces. In fact, you may know how they feel by looking at them before they are even aware of it. They light up when they speak, but their facial expressions go flat when they move.

Although VAKs maintain nearly constant eye contact while listening, they often will look away and up to think and find their words. They have to close their eyes to know how they feel or what they want to do.

Language Characteristics

In general, VAK children are very social, "people people," who love to talk with their many friends and acquaintances. Upon entering any room of people, they typically look around for someone to talk to.

VAKs can be very articulate. They have a lot of energy and feeling in their words. Hand gestures sometimes follow what they say if they want to emphasize a point. They like to teach and explain things, and love to tell stories in great detail, using lots of visual metaphors to paint pictures for their listeners. Kids with the VAK pattern can be very persuasive with their words, trying to convince adults and children alike to see things their way. When they speak, they tend to use visual vocabulary—

words that present images—words like "see, look, colorful, show," and "bright," and phrases like "I can see your point," and "See you later." They often use fillers, like "um," "like," or "you know" between thoughts.

VAK children are often quite good at back and forth dialogue. They can hold their own in most rapid conversations with another person. They often find it useful to think out loud with someone else in order to decide between two options or to discover their own opinion about something.

It is easy for these kids to hear both sides of any story. Sometimes this is frustrating for those listening; they may say one thing one day, say something different the next day, and mean both. They can also do two auditory activities, like listening to the radio and talking on the phone, at the same time.

When asked about their feelings, the pace of a VAK's language will slow down considerably. Some will be hesitant to speak at all unless they feel safe and comfortable with their questioner. You can often tell a lot about how your VAK child feels by the tone of his or her voice.

These children feel what they hear on a deep level. Abrasive noises or harsh tones of voice can have a significant effect on their emotional state. Music can change their mood or their energy level; it can help calm or energize them, deflate or inspire them.

Physical Characteristics

VAK children usually have a very sketchy sense of their bodies. At times, they may even forget they have one! They can sit for very long periods of time without moving. They may be aware of how their body feels as a whole, but it is very difficult for them to pinpoint sensations. They may know their leg hurts without being able to tell or show you the exact location of the pain.

Children with the VAK pattern are often hesitant to compete physically. They usually prefer activities they can do in a free-form way, like walking, swinging, biking, swimming, or skiing. They may choose to stay indoors at recess to read or help out.

It may be difficult for VAK kids to learn structured physical activities. This is the place these children feel the most "disabled" in the schooling process. They may feel clumsy, awkward, and self-conscious in learning with their hands and bodies.

VAKs can get impatiently bored doing a repetitive activity. They will add their own unique variations rather than do the same thing in the same way over and over. For this reason, they may have trouble staying with the same task for a long period of time. To offset boredom, they will often go from one activity to another and then back to the first. They may change their minds frequently, even in the middle of something they've chosen to do. They sometimes have difficulty finishing tasks. This may be, in part, because they have a hard time estimating the amount of time it takes to do something.

Touch is not a casual thing for children with this pattern. Physical contact, both positive and negative, has a profound impact on them. VAKs tend to be quite shy about any kind of touch unless they know you quite well. Invasive touch can be difficult for them to cope with and can leave a harmful, lasting impression.

VAKs are children who feel things very deeply, but are very private about their feelings. They are often affected by words that convey emotion. When they are angry, they may express it with a dirty look, a visual gesture, or by writing a nasty note.

VAKs get confused and space out when they are given too many choices of what to do, when they are asked questions about how they feel, how to do something, how they have done something, or when they are touched.

VAK Portrait

"Cathy was a `model student' in one of my fifth grade classes," remembers Anne. "I actually felt sort of useless at times as her teacher. She entered fifth grade with all of her basic skills well in hand, reading above grade level, knowing all the basic facts and processes in math, and writing with skill and creativity. She kept her desk neat, her papers were well-organized and on time, and I never had trouble reading her handwriting. She was the one the other kids looked at when no one else knew the answer. Cathy's academic world was one of mostly holding herself back, so that she wouldn't look too smart, or be called a goodie-goodie, so that she'd fit in.

"The most remarkable time I remember with her was when she approached me about doing a science project. She had read in a book somewhere about how an egg becomes a chick, and was curious enough to get some eggs from a local farm and some help from her parents in building an incubator. She wanted to know if the class could assist her with the process, since the eggs needed to be turned twice a day. For eight weeks, we were the custodians of a half dozen eggs. Cathy sparkled as she taught us how to tend those eggs. She helped us imagine what was happening inside those small shells. Hatching day was a miracle indeed. Cathy's learning literally came alive for her, and for all of us."

Communicating with VAK Children

Supporting Their Visual Channel

VAKs want most to be seen and heard, and to be appreciated for what they've read, what they've written, and what they've created visually. They love mail, both sending and receiving it. Send them letters, cards, and pictures; leave them little notes in surprising places. Encourage them to write to friends and relatives. They get great pleasure from writing something that someone else will read.

Writing will also help VAK kids bring their thinking into focus. Have a conversation on paper with them, especially if they seem confused about something. Introduce them to the benefits of keeping a journal. Encourage them to write themselves reminders: what they want to do, to read, to buy, to say, or to learn. Help them find a place to put these lists so they can see them when they feel overwhelmed by choices. Also encourage them to write down what they have done so they can see it. This will help them stay aware of their accomplishments.

If you want them to remember something, leave them a note. Giving them both written and verbal instructions may be most effective.

Understand that how things look is very important to VAK children. Tell them when you notice that they've straightened up their rooms. Help them find the styles and colors in clothes that reflect their most positive self-image. Tell them the effect that looking at them has on you.

Eye contact is important to VAKs. You know you have their attention when they're looking at you, but don't expect them to maintain it indefinitely—they need to look up and away while thinking; their eyes help them to find their words. Your facial expressions communicate a lot to your VAK child.

Encourage your VAK children to explore the richness of metaphor. For example, find out how their week has been with a question like "Has it been like a ship on the water or like a roller coaster?" VAKs are curious about the patterns in their lives; using metaphor can help them explore these patterns in a creative, meaningful way.

Supporting Their Auditory Channel

VAK children often need a lot of time to talk through the experiences of their lives: what they've done, how they feel, what they like, or what's hard for them. They may not fully know how they feel about anything until they talk about all sides of a given issue. Often they don't want advice or agreement. They just want air time. Invite them to tell you what they are thinking and then listen.

VAKs love being interviewed, dialoguing back and forth, and helping others work through problems verbally. Sit face to face with them. Ask them expansive, curious questions. Tell them the effect their words are having on you. Be truthful, even about hard feelings. Explain things to them using metaphor and analogy. Be patient and *don't* interrupt when they tell you what they are feeling. Since this comes from a very deep place, their words will be slower, with more pauses. They may have to close their eyes or look up to find what they want to say.

Supporting Their Kinesthetic Channel

VAK children feel things deeply. Offer them quiet moments of just being with them as they tune in to their bodies and emotions. Allow them time to express what's going on, not only in words but in tears, laughter, or body movements. Please do not tell VAKs what they are feeling. If you notice an expression, tone of voice, or body posture that makes you curious, ask them about it.

Do things together at their rhythm, if possible. Help them to learn how long it takes them to do something. Please ask rather than tell them what to do. Avoid doing things for them. Give them clear time boundaries for accomplishing something and let them know the consequences of their not finishing on time.

Be patient in teaching VAKs physical skills. Invite them, don't force them to learn anything in this realm. Teach them your way as one possibility. Then, be open to their adapting what you've taught them into their own way. Verbally praise them for their efforts and their progress. Encourage them to practice what they are learning on their own, at their own rate. Allow them to be private about their new skill as long as they need to be.

Support your VAK children to follow through on doing what they say they are going to do. Create a chart, list, or diagram which will visually remind them of their commitments. Encourage them to set reasonable expectations for themselves so they can have the satisfaction of completion. Help them to break large tasks down into smaller, manageable parts. Make sure they include some variety or rotation in their expected responsibilities. They may not be consistent if they must stick to an invariable routine. Help them find phrases or pictures that will motivate them into action; place these motivators where they will see them often. Encourage them to give themselves visual and verbal credit for each accomplishment. Make sure they reward themselves when they reach completion.

Helping VAKs at Home

Of all children, VAKs may appear to need the least amount of outside help from you at home. They tend to do well in school primarily because traditional teaching styles, which are largely "show and tell," match their learning pattern and meet their most basic educational needs. It may be however, that their learning process does not go deeply enough: VAKs can easily cram for a test, score well, and not retain what they have "learned" over time. What's missing too often is what makes learning come alive for all of us—the kinesthetic, experiential component. If your child is a VAK learner, don't confuse A's on his or her report card with a satisfactory learning experience.

As parents, you can most effectively support the complete integration of your children's learning by finding ways for them to get enthusiastically involved in what they are studying. Perhaps the best way for you to do this is to join them. Take an interest in what they are learning even though they can generally work competently on most typical assignments by themselves. Set aside time to talk about their special interests. Expand their experience of academic subjects whenever possible, and have fun! If they are studying astronomy, for example, take a trip to the planetarium, have a star named after your child, or sleep out under the stars together on a clear night.

Read together. Read to them or have them read to you out loud. With older VAKs, occasionally read a book they've been assigned along with them and discuss it together.

Take time to listen to what these children have written. It helps them to edit effectively if they can hear the flow of their words out loud.

VAKs may not be able to think with visual clutter. Help them set up a work space that they can keep relatively neat. Encourage them to include just enough color and things to look at without being distracting. Provide a special place to display your VAK's accomplishments, doodles, winning score sheets from a card game marathon, or photos.

Support VAKs in their speaking and teaching. Invite them to tell their favorite stories. Share yours with them. Practice debating with them. They will start out being able to understand and agree with both sides. Talking out what they think will help them discover what's true for them.

One easy way for VAK children to get overwhelmed is with the use of time. They tend to procrastinate and often cannot judge accurately how long a specific task will take. Just as with other responsibilities, help them to break down projects or papers into smaller tasks and to set realistic deadlines. Encourage them to plan variety into their timelines. Again, don't forget progress charts, motivators, and rewards.

In working on projects, VAKs can imagine in elaborate detail something their hands cannot create easily. Encourage these kids to plan simple presentations.

VAKs frequently think and write well with a computer. It helps them keep track of many visual details and allows them to write and edit easily. If possible, encourage them to become computer literate early.

◆ ◆ ◆

In summary, with these children who want to illuminate the whole world, the most important things you can give them are a place to shine brightly, a patient ear as they explore their feelings, and encouragement to go deeply enough to discover their sense of purpose and vision.

11

Going With the Grain: Utilizing Differences in the Classroom

"Education is not filling a vessel, but lighting a fire."

—Carl Jung

Once the basics of this approach to understanding how children learn are explained, the question that is asked more than any other is, "But there are thirty children in a classroom— children may learn in many different ways, but how does a teacher manage to teach them all?"

It's quite possible to teach students of all six patterns in one classroom, but it takes a willingness to accept that different instruments play the same music in different ways. Understanding perceptual processing also means we must change the way we think about how to teach and what the role of the teacher really is. In this chapter, we'll explore how the challenges that diversity brings can be used to create an effective and alive education for all children.

Teaching as an Art Form

A teacher is an artist. And what media could be more important than the human mind? Teachers who are most effective approach their work in ways very similar to sculptors or cabinet makers. They don't try to control the wood. They know that every piece has a different grain and that you have to work with the grain instead of against it. Fine teachers strive to understand and respect the individual nature and strength of each child's mind and design his or her learning accordingly.

In Japanese it is not possible to say, "I am looking at the child." You can only say, "The child and I are looking at each other." Thus, you also cannot say, "I am teaching the child." Even if you try, it would still come out, "The child and I are teaching each other."

Children are experts in learning. What can they teach us about wonder, creativity, compassion? What can our children teach us about how they learn and what they need to learn more effectively? In order to be fully effective, learning should be full of discoveries for *both* the teacher and student. It's simply a matter of conceiving of education in a slightly different way.

Let's think of the source of learning as if it were a flashlight on a miner's hat. If the teacher is perceived as the source of all learning, then the light shines out from him or her onto all the children who are its focus. But what if we assume there is a light inside each child and the teacher's task is to figure out how to help a child turn his or hers on? That would mean the teacher's job would be more like coaching or guiding.

Putting the lights back on the kids' hats where they belong means thinking of education as a participative process. It means offering students choices about what they learn, how they will learn, and how they will demonstrate and evaluate what they have learned.

Children don't resist change. They resist *being* changed. You don't need to change what you are doing with them, but you do need to change *how* you are doing it. Common sense tells you that learning how to drive a car comes before learning where to go in one. This means that children have to be taught how their minds work as soon as possible in their school life. It wouldn't be difficult to get kids interested in the subject either. All children want to know as much as possible about the mysterious world inside themselves.

One of the best ways of discovering someone's thinking pattern is to have them teach you something. "Listen, Mrs. Jamison, just tell yourself you can do it, and then put your hands on the bat and get a good grip. Yeah, Great! Now feel your knees sinking and count while the pitcher winds up . . . ." Mrs. Jamison now knows that Joshua uses auditory information to organize, kinesthetic to sort, and visual (which was never mentioned) to create. Thus she can put him with the kids that are learning their spelling words by making up chants and movements to go with them. She can have Joshua help Simon, who is verbally shy but visually quite active, create posters and advertising slogans for the class business.

The exploration of the learning process needs to be woven into the fabric of what students are taught. Our advocacy for them can only go so far. If they know how their minds work, they can be their own best advocates. Imagine Celeste saying to her science teacher, "I understand what you just said, but I need a visual to really be able to apply it. Would you please draw me diagram, Mr. Scapula, so I can get it?" Students can be engaged in their own learning in such a way that they can say what they want to know and help adults teach it to them.

We all need to learn how to learn together. The violence in our society clearly indicates that we need skills training in how to relate to one another and how to work collaboratively. Businesses are learning that using teams is more efficient, effective, and produces higher quality. But most of us have been taught only to compete, not to collaborate. What children like most about coming to school, about summer vacation, about recess and extracurricular activities is being with their friends. To children, playing and learning are the same thing. It is only in school they are made to be different. The more you enjoy doing something, the more engaged and effective you will be. Why not go with that grain instead of against it?

What if children help each other turn on their lights? Anyone who comes from a large family knows that kids teaching each other works. Often times, the most important things we ever learn are learned from peers. What if children of like thinking patterns are clustered together and are guided by the teacher to learn the multiplication tables? The KAVs might build a boat with six- and seven-inch pieces of wood; the VKAs might draw up plans for a bridge; the VAKs might make up stories about Six and Sevenland which the AKVs might act out. The KVAs could quietly collect leaves with seven edges and the AVKs could make up cheers.

We need to think about learning in terms of relationships: how can you help your children relate to their own minds, to each other, to their teachers, to you? How can you relate to your children as if you were a mentor who cares about their spirits, as a coach who leads without bossing? How can you relate to their capacities as differences, not deficits? How can you relate to teachers as colleagues on the same side? How can you help teachers relate to their own minds so they will understand how best to communicate what they have to offer?

Putting it into Practice

For the last several years, many people have been asking me to develop a standardized test that would determine a child's learning pattern. In the beginning, I responded by gnashing my teeth, rolling my eyes heavenward and groaning. To put it mildly, I am not fond of timed, machine scored, fill-in-the-blanks standardized tests. They never test what they are supposed to, they don't tell you the things you need to know to teach someone something, and most importantly of all, they are radically inaccurate for children whose minds follow the AKV and KAV pattern. That means they do not determine what *at least* one-third of all children who are given the test know or have learned. They are best for determining how smart the people are who designed the test. If I didn't know what I know about learning patterns, any test I designed would be accurate for VAKs, but the KAVs would all score in the bottom percentile.

"Standardized" (as used in this kind of test) and "individualized" are a contradiction in terms. An expensive and harmful contradiction. When I taught fifth grade in Hanover, New Hampshire, I found a little $5 book called *Deal Me In*, which was written by a gifted teacher. It taught adults how to discover the perceptual aptitudes of children by playing various card games with them for an hour or so. Even as I devoured it from cover to cover, the man who was then the school psychologist was bringing the children who were "learning disabled" into his office to administer a standardized test that did the same thing but cost several hundred dollars to purchase, took three hours to give, two hours to score, and another hour to write up an evaluation report. Paralysis by analysis!

For a moment, you be the school psychologist. What do you think was really going on with "hyperactive" Butch who couldn't sit still in class? Or distractible Dora who kept staring out of the window during creative writing class? Or "oppositional" Fred who didn't answer his French teacher when called on to conjugate the verb *avoir*?

Instead of spending the first week of every school year having children mark between the dotted lines of those endless computer answer sheets with number two pencils, instead of waiting for months to get useless test results that go into a child's permanent cumulative folder, instead of all of that controlled compartmentalization, imagine this as the beginning of your child's school year:

A week in which teachers and students and parents are mutually curious and observant about how each child learns. Perhaps there are sheets of newsprint on all the walls with a child's name at the top of each one. Anyone who discovers anything about the learning capacities and preferences of that child—family members, the janitor, the coach, friend—can write the information on the paper. Sharing the process, sharing the excitement when eight-year-old Butch comes up to Mrs. Rettenhauser exclaiming, "Guess what? I think I learn through my hands and body really well 'cause Marvin taught me how to cut up a frog and I learned it real easy. Now I wanna draw all about it." An interactive, participatory, first week when curiosity reigns supreme. (In fact, it could be the fifth or thirty-fifth week.) The only cost is the price of a pad of newsprint.

Let's go into a fourth grade classroom on a Thursday afternoon in March during spelling practice time. In a typical class, all students would have studied the same words in the same way--writing them down, making up sentences that contain those words, writing them down again, and then saying the letters over and over in their minds. (Guess the pattern of the teacher who thought up that method a hundred years ago—VAK!)

Since it is Thursday, everyone is numbering half sheets of blue lined white paper for the practice test. If all twenty words are spelled correctly today, the student doesn't have to re-take the test tomorrow. The year could be 1942 or 1992. The teacher and the curriculum provided her by the district are the source, the boss. Everyone is taught the same thing in the same way. The kids that are "good spellers" do well, the others try to work harder or give up on spelling altogether. Which may also mean they give up on creative writing because some teachers have been instructed to put as much emphasis on spelling as content. Which may also mean they give up on English and language skills altogether.

But let's visit the same classroom and assume the teacher knows all about thinking patterns and has been encouraged and supported to teach interactively. It is spelling practice time and the room is alive with activity. Each child has his or her own list of words to study which have come from whatever stories he or she has been writing as well as science projects. They're spread around the room in pairs, small groups, and solos. Two VAKs are making a drawing out of the words in colored ink. A small group of AVKs are in a corner having their own spelling bee. A pair of VKAs are at the chalkboard where one is trying to find the errors intentionally written into the list by the other. Two KVAs are working together, writing out the words they feel their partner scribbling on their backs, while four or five others work alone on the computers developing spelling games for the rest of the class. A group of AKVs are outside making up cheers as they jump rope and some KAVs are tossing a ball back and forth as they recite each other's words.

All of these children will experience success in spelling this week. They will be learning to spell words that are important and mean something to them. The teacher acts as a guide to help insure a positive experience for each child: the words learned are within stretch range, not beyond reach. The options provided maximize the possibility of success since they are tailored to specific thinking patterns. Students will be given the opportunity to be involved in the decisions about when they will be ready to be evaluated and what form that will take. In this classroom, the teacher and students are collaborators, sharing the responsibility, fun, excitement, and satisfaction of learning. No one needs to fail, including the teacher.

General Guidelines

What follows is not meant to be a list of comprehensive recommendations for revamping methods of instruction. These ideas are given as an illustration of how an awareness of perceptual processing can influence how we teach and learn. The place to start, the most basic guideline of all is this: Learning will be most effective if every lesson taught includes an auditory, visual, and kinesthetic component in how information is conveyed. In other words, knowledge should be transmitted by reading and demonstration, through action, and by verbal instruction.

Let's suppose the subject is weather prediction. A trip to a local TV weather station would certainly provide all three. Most likely, someone would be available to explain the processes involved in making a forecast. The kids could see and, hopefully, touch sample instruments. The experience of being in the environment where weather prediction happens will make it come alive for them.

If this is not possible, kids could listen to weather forecasts, read about, and learn how to use familiar weather instruments, like thermometers and barometers. Again, all three perceptual modes would be involved. Too often what happens is that teachers resort to simply having students read about the process in a textbook. It quickly becomes obvious what elements are missing and which kinds of learners get left behind.

Equally important is the expressive side of the learning process, how children demonstrate that they have learned the material at hand. Again, options should be given that include all three channels. Our students of weather might create their own weather station back in the classroom. They might give oral reports on the conditions that lead up to specific kinds of severe weather. They might chart present conditions on a graph and monitor how close their predictions come to what really happens. These options may seem fairly ordinary and obvious. Yet, in an average classroom, how often are all of them offered? Again, how often, due to lack of materials and preparation time, or due to mistaken assumptions, do teachers require all students to prove what they have learned on a written test?

The more channels that can be incorporated into how the information is presented and the more options provided for presenting the learning that has taken place, the more involved the kids will be, the more they will be motivated, the more relevant it will feel, and the easier teaching and learning will be. It is important for teachers to remember that their students' responses to offerings in all three channels will differ greatly. It might be fun for an AKV to give an oral report or teach something to a small group. For a VKA, on the other hand, this same option will be a real stretch. Children with the KAV pattern may come alive with a hands-on science project, while an AVK may need special attention through the process, perhaps feeling clumsy and unsure of himself.

Perceptual processing will help teachers more fully understand some of the typical, frustrating behaviors in the classroom as indications of learning needs. When kids fidget or space out, it can signal to teachers that it is time to change the mode of learning or expressing; they may need to include more movement or fewer words in what they are presenting or requesting.

Teachers should encourage students to build confidence in learning by using their front channel when possible. The strength of this part of their minds should also be used to support the less accessible parts when they are called on in a learning situation. For example, AKV children, whose speaking prowess is evident, can use their voices to study spelling. Writing spelling words over and over can be tedious and not especially effective for them, but they will remember much more easily words they have spelled out loud in a sing-song fashion.

Special attention needs to be given to each child's unconscious channel as well. Teachers must remain aware of the challenges that the slow-paced mode of the unconscious mind presents in every learning situation. In evaluation, provide extra encouragement and open-ended options for those students who take the risk to express themselves from this tender and uniquely creative place.

Children whose unconscious channel is kinesthetic, for example, should be supported to take all the time they need when learning movement patterns, working in shop, etc., and encouraged to compete with themselves rather than other students. Similarly, students whose minds use the visual unconscious channel should be allowed to take written assignments home or estimate how much time they think they'll need. And for those whose minds use auditory in their unconscious, encourage them to have a visual model to refer to when they speak, and provide opportunities where they can speak to one or two other children rather than the whole class.

In the learning process, there is no way to avoid presenting information in someone's unconscious channel, nor is that necessarily desirable. By encouraging students for whom this is so to keep a channel further to the front of their mind in action during this time, you ensure they will be able to pay attention.

We all do this naturally, though typical ways of trying to keep ourselves alert are usually thought of as frustrating habits. Annoyances are often good coping behaviors. When Steve, VKA, fiddles with his hair or rolls his pencil around, his teachers may not be aware that these small kinesthetic activities are actually helping him pay better attention to what they are saying.

If we can understand the need underneath the behavior, we no longer have to try to control or eliminate it. We can use it; we can point out to Steve the usefulness of what he's doing and help him find more effective, perhaps less distracting ways of getting this need met. For example, he might be interested in bringing in a tennis ball which he could squeeze and strengthen his grip with while listening.

In every person's pattern, there are two channels which don't connect directly, the conscious and the unconscious. This is where the importance of the subconscious channel really is evident. Teachers aware of this missing link can help their students fill it in. VAKs, for example, are generally not skilled at things which require good eye-hand coordination, because there is no direct connection between the visual and kinesthetic channels in their pattern. Therefore, the middle auditory channel is crucial in learning to do something with their hands or their bodies—they need to talk themselves through these kinds of activities in order to complete the link.

In a similar way, VKAs may have difficulty learning how to read orally, an activity which requires them to say what they see. The kinesthetic channel can help complete this circuit for children of this pattern. It may be crucial for them to follow what they are reading with a finger, to stand up, use their hands, or move around when it is their turn.

As you can see, once you understand the fundamentals of thinking patterns, meeting each child's individual educational needs is just a matter of being flexible.

Bored and Bossed

The two things that children of all ages complain about is that they feel bored and bossed in school. But not in all situations. And not always. In extracurricular activities, for instance, they rarely complain about either.

Let's take these complaints one at a time, bored first. Bored equals frustrated. Children learn by asking themselves, in effect,

"What? (. . . is this about?)"; "So What? (How is it relevant to me?)"; "Now What? (Can I learn it and can I use it?)" If they can't answer all of those questions, they will be frustrated and probably say they are bored.

The language of boredom is often a smokescreen for the way children think about themselves. "This is dumb. Do I hafta do it?" equals "I'm dumb. I'm afraid I won't be able to do this." Often they "can't" learn because the information is not presented in the way their mind absorbs it most easily.

Even as a kindergartner, Anne's son Brian sometimes says that school is boring. When she probes a little deeper, he actually means he doesn't want to try because he is afraid he will fail. More often than not, the things he finds "boring" are related to his back channel: activities which require him (AKV) to focus visually on detail, which is not comfortable for his learning pattern.

Remember, a child's brain is a learning/surviving machine. It is designed to learn and produce. Depression, hurting, getting sick, being miserable are all attempts to relieve frustration. If children are not able to do what they are being asked to do, it's necessary to break it down into manageable pieces or to find another way to teach them. There's no more point in trying to make children do what they believe they can't than in trying to get a factory worker to lift what he cannot budge. It's necessary to encourage them to go from comfort to stretch, but not to stress. It isn't necessary to motivate them. Discovering that they can do quality work will motivate them.

We need to put the flashlights back on the kids' hats where they belong. We need to turn toward intrinsic motivation and evaluation, which means teaching material that is useful, relevant, tangible, and palpable to children and involving them in figuring out how they know when it's mastered. If what is being taught isn't relevant to the child, then it is the teacher's responsibility to find a way it can be. Set up a class store to explain principles of economics. Have them learn about biographies by writing ones for Madonna or the school principal. Have them create a plot for their favorite Saturday morning cartoon characters and submit it to the station. If what has to be learned isn't interesting, the students can be asked how they could learn it in a way that would be.

Children can always be given choices, for instance, to demonstrate what they have learned by constructing something with their hands or writing a report or making an oral presentation. Teachers can give children an experience, tell them stories, give them hand-outs, or direct them to books to read. The more effectively the information is communicated, the less time is spent dealing with Jennifer's clowning and Samuel's whining.

Adults expect children to be adaptable, while we are very unadaptable ourselves. It is we who should be flexible since we have more experience and know more options. We are the ones who should be expected to find new ways of maneuvering around obstacles, rather than trying to manipulate children over them.

In reading, books should be chosen by the child, be lively, and in language they are likely to use. The skills of writing should be taught through students' imaginative writing and written descriptions about their own experiences rather than through drills and rote.

In math, instruction should be related to real world problems, with children learning at their own pace and structuring solutions in their own way. Instead of mastering arithmetic first, it is more effective to integrate fractions, algebra, geometry, and statistics skills at every level. In science, an emphasis should be put on practical applications before the abstract (ie., fourth graders fixing irons and toasters, sixth graders developing solar powered toys).

High school students should be given the option to live out their learnings more fully by being involved in apprenticeship programs which are integrated into their curriculum. Both students and teachers need to be supported and encouraged to find ways to put fun and interest in their work. Perhaps then our worries about test scores and dropout rates will become irrelevant.

And what about children feeling "bossed" in school? Look around the average high school classroom. Give various objects in it a voice—what message do they convey? To me, the chalkboard says, "Look this way, everything important will happen here." The hard chairs say, "Don't get too comfortable. Sit still." The desks in rows say, "Be like everyone else." The clock says, "Finish when I tell you." The walls say, "Be numb. Don't get too excited." The lights say, "The world is harsh. Be artificial. Speed up."

Enter another classroom with us. This one belongs to David Ely in Hinesburg, Vermont, who believes that biology means the study of living things and that his role is to ignite his students' desire to learn. Two sides of the room are crowded with aquariums and terrariums filled with harvester ants, a tarantula, African clawed toads, a fifteen-foot python, and more. On the third, there is a solid screen of plants, and a row of computers. The walls are covered with books, posters, and models. What does this classroom say to you?

School children are given very few choices about how to use their minds, what to learn, or when to learn it. When given only one way, the teacher's way, to learn and demonstrate what they know, many students' educational needs go unmet. By insisting on being "the bosses" in our one-way-or-else approach, educators are fostering failure and alienating the very people they are supposed to serve. Traditionally, bosses never give up power and are always seeking more. They run things from the top down. Businesses all over the world are learning that effectiveness in the twenty-first century will require that leaders share power and continue to seek better ways to do this. It's time for schools to catch up.

What we have offered in this chapter goes beyond the concepts of a new way to teach and learn. We have laid out a very specific plan of action. The changes we are suggesting do not require any more money from the budget or sophisticated tests or new kits. What their implementation does require, however, is the willingness to be adaptable and the courage to make room for curiosity and collaboration in every aspect of the teaching-learning process. It will take all of us together to transform schools from places where children feel bossed and bored into places where they learn to trust their minds, from dead classrooms where things feel square, brown, and stiff into alive spaces that welcome the things inside your child that need expressing.

Unique In The Same Way As Everyone Else

We love the following piece, which we've both carried around for years. Although the author is unknown to us, what happened to the child is all too familiar.

He always wanted to say things. But no one understood. He always wanted to explain things. But no one cared. He would lie out on the grass and look up in the sky. It would be only him and the sky and the things inside that needed saying. And it was after that that he drew the picture. It was a beautiful picture. He kept it under his pillow and let no one see it. He looked at it every night and thought about it. When it was dark and his eyes were closed, he could still see it. And it was all of him. And he loved it.

When he started school, he brought it with him. Not to show anyone, but just to have with him like a friend. It was funny about school. He sat at a square, brown desk like all the other square, brown desks and he thought it should be red. And his room was a square, brown room. Like all the other rooms. And it was tight, and close, and stiff. He hated to hold the pencil and the chalk with his arm stiff and his feet flat on the floor, stiff, with the teacher watching and watching.

Then he had to write numbers. And they weren't anything. They were worse than the letters that could be something if you put them together. And the numbers were tight and square and he hated the whole thing.

The teacher came and spoke to him. She told him to wear a tie like all the other boys. He said he didn't like them and she said it didn't matter. After that, they drew. And he drew all yellow and it was the way he felt that morning. And it was beautiful. The teacher came and smiled at him. "What's this?" said she. "Why can't you draw something like Ken's drawing? Isn't that beautiful?" It was all questions.

Then his mother bought him a tie and he drew airplanes and rocket ships like everyone else. He threw the old picture away. When he lay out alone looking at the sky, it was big and blue and all of everything, but he wasn't anymore. He was square inside and brown, and his hands were stiff. He was like anyone else. And the thing inside him that needed saying didn't need saying anymore. It had stopped pushing. It was crushed still. Like everything else.

12

Collaborating to Create A Possible Future

> *"Never doubt that a small group of thoughtful, committed citizens can change the world; indeed, it's the only thing that ever has."*
>
> —Margaret Mead

Once upon a time, a blind man got lost in an immense forest. He wandered from tree to tree totally disoriented, until he came to a clearing. There he fumbled around, finally tripping over something, a tree root he supposed, and was knocked down to the ground. Grasping it, he fumbled to pull himself up, and heard, "Ouch." It seemed it wasn't a root at all, but the foot of an old crippled woman who was lying on the forest floor.

"I beg your pardon," said the blind man, "Who are you and what are you doing here?"

The crippled woman gasped, "I have been here for a very long time. It seems like forever. I cannot walk. Thus I have been lying here waiting to die."

The blind man brushed himself off and stood up. "I too have been here a very long time, wandering around, lost and alone, trying to find my way out." Both of them sighed in despair, until the old woman called out, "I've got an idea. Why don't you lift me up on your shoulders and carry me out. I can see and guide us both!"

Delighted, the blind man followed her instructions and together they found their way out of the forest.

◆ ◆ ◆

Parents and teachers contain the pressures of so much these days. We often find ourselves lost in the educational forest of powerlessness and despair. Will it collapse and divide us into adversaries or will we use it to stretch us into a new alliance of power and vision that will lead our children into the twenty-first century?

In this chapter, I'd like to offer you some guidelines for forming such an alliance so that you can help implement what you've learned about how your children's minds work and be effective in extending that knowledge to their schools. Since a parent must begin and end as an advocate for his or her child, I hope this chapter will support you in finding both the courage to make yourself understood as well as the compassion to understand what it is to be a classroom teacher in today's world.

Lost in the Forest

Parents want to find a way to make a difference in their children's education, a way in, and teachers want to find a way to reach out. But all too often these days, they find themselves at opposite ends of the forest. Let's begin from the perspective of the classroom teacher. What I'm about to share is only one of what I'm sure could be a thousand similar stories.

My husband and I taught a weekend workshop last month on the East Coast. One of the participants, Mario, had been a high school teacher for ten years in one of the worst schools in the city. He was six feet, nine inches tall. His mind used the VKA pattern. When I think of him, the words that come to mind are invincibly tender. We talked a lot about his job, the kids he taught, why he loved them and how hard it was because there wasn't enough for them: he didn't have enough books for all of them; they had to wear their coats in class because there wasn't enough heat; there weren't enough of the services they desperately needed such as drug rehab programs.

After the lunch break we played "In the Living Years" by Mike and the Mechanics. Andy went over and sat silently next to Mario, who began to cry. He had just received a phone call that one of his students had been caught in crossfire on the school basketball court and was killed. He held his head in his hands and whispered over and over, "I don't think I can take it anymore. I don't think I can take it anymore."

On the two days following the workshop, we were hired by the person in charge of teacher training for the school system who had gotten a grant so that we could conduct a seminar on thinking patterns. I was amazed when only eleven special service personnel showed up. The principals said there wasn't enough money to pay for faculty to have substitute teachers that day, since they had attended a workshop the previous month about new state regulations.

The building in which our seminar was held was huge, brand new, and devoted entirely to administration. It was overflowing with "enough." There was not a single child to be found, but there were sixty sumptuous offices for personnel in various positions with various titles. The room where we taught was filled with expensive audio-visual equipment including a $1,500 board that had replaced $4.95 newsprint flipcharts. It even had a built-in copier so the people in meetings wouldn't have to take notes. (Mario had told me there wasn't one single copying machine in his entire school that served 2,000 students!)

This incident isn't unique to this one city. Teachers all over the country are frustrated. A woman who teaches science in

Colorado called me a few weeks ago and insisted, "I hate BIG! What's wrong with this country is that everything is divided in pieces that are too *big*. My classes are too big. I'm teaching so many kids, it takes me a month to even remember their names. How can I teach a child I have to keep calling, `Hey you'?!"

A furious math teacher from San Diego called to tell me her school system had just spent all of their materials budget for the year on a "new system" that was supposed to be the ultimate solution to increasing math scores. It proudly advertised it had a "strong" kinesthetic element—children got to *hold* their flash cards!

There are teachers in every school who intuitively sense that each child learns differently. Why aren't those teachers being fostered? Why aren't *they* in charge of training, program development, and purchasing instead of being corseted into using expensive materials that don't work? Who develops these ornate materials anyway? Why aren't school systems interested in indigenous, generic methods originated by classroom teachers?

Anne's experience confirms the frustration: "I have been stuck on both sides of the forest. As a teacher, I was intensely curious about the students that I taught. As thirty-one of them entered my classroom each September, I knew I needed the trust and partnership of their parents in order to teach them effectively. On Open School Night, I asked mothers and fathers to write down anything they knew about their children that might help me: how they learned, their talents, skills, and interests. Much to my surprise, I got very little information back. Now I understand that those parents couldn't believe that their everyday knowledge, their own experience, would be valuable to me, the expert. At all costs, they wanted to avoid presenting their child as a problem or as one with no problems at all. Trust between teachers and parents had become so deeply eroded, they didn't feel comfortable responding to a simple question to which they had valuable answers.

"As a parent, with the intensity of a typical new mother, I was fascinated by my own son Brian's AKV approach to the world. With my understanding of thinking patterns, I set aside expectations of what he should be like, and felt wonderfully curious about everything he did. I was delighted with his love of words and how quickly he learned them. Instead of expecting him to be "boyishly" physically skilled from the start, I companioned him patiently as he found his own unique way of safely taking physical chances. I noticed how long he could get lost in a picture that captured his attention. Understanding about thinking patterns helped me support his natural ways of learning.

"Even with a full five years of getting to know his talents and preferences, what things he learns with ease and what frustrates him, as he entered a public school kindergarten, I found myself anxious on the other side of the classroom door. I was terrified that my son's natural love of life and learning would be destroyed by 'the system.' And I felt powerless in the face of this possibility. Even with all I've studied, I have been reluctant to be too forthcoming with information about Brian and how he learns. I tell myself I don't want to be too pushy or to present myself as an expert, even about my own child, because I'm afraid it will alienate or annoy his teacher and backfire on him.

"I feel within me the leftovers of a very old assumption: that parents and teachers are adversaries in a very important contest and that I must, for the sake of my child, defer to the learning 'experts.' So I hand him silently over to the system and pray, pray that 'they' won't destroy him, pray they will feed his mind rather than wound it, pray they will know him as I know him."

The Meeting Place

Anne is not alone. When most parents enter the classroom for the first parent-teacher conference of the year and sit in that little chair next to the big desk, they seem to erase what they know about their children like a wet sponge on a chalkboard. Even though they are adults, they forget how *they're* smart.

Schools are organized to teach us to put our center of balance in the expert—in the teacher, the principal, the learning specialist. We are taught not to know whether we're good learners unless we get a certain grade that says so. We don't know how long we can spend at doing something or whether it interests us because we're so trained into being directed by an external source—when the bell rings that's when we're finished with a project, not when something inside tells us.

As adults, most of us have had at least twelve years of training at putting our centers of balance outside in the teachers. As soon as we get into our child's classroom, the response is retriggered that someone on the outside knows more than we know. We unconsciously are working out of a defensive and vulnerable position. Schools teach us to be reactive instead of proactive.

Everyone of us is, in fact, a teacher. We all teach people something—how to work the stamp machine, plant bulbs in a garden, mend socks, etc. When you go to a conference in your child's school, remembering that there is a teacher who lives in you helps keep your center of balance inside yourself.

Children are also teachers, but they are usually absent from these conferences, even though it is their learning, lives, minds, excitement, and difficulties that are being discussed. It makes me think of the small carved statues of women in China called "Doctor Dolls": the woman's husband would take it to the doctor and point to the places his wife was in pain, describing her symptoms as best he could. Not the most direct way to heal what's wrong!

Children today need mentors, people who care about and support their spirits. Parents and teachers can learn to form a mentoring alliance. Its focus is simple: How can you help your children learn to trust their own minds, love learning, and do quality work? Rather than attribute achievement to innate ability that some have and some don't, we should expect that all children can learn, given the right instruction and environment.

The product of education is not better schools, but students who are learning better. Therefore, the subject of the conference should be how your child can be most effectively taught. Rather than being an object we are talking about and doing things to, he or she should be an integral part of this alliance. Consider telling your child's teacher you would like him or her to be present. Once there, the common denominator should be how *is* your child smart, how do we access all of his abilities? What are her assets and how can they be used?

You must advocate for your children in school. You know things about them that no one else knows. You can begin by remembering that it is natural for children to learn. Their brains are learning machines. Most kids learn more in recess and summer vacations than they do in school. We need to explore the environment that for any particular child maximizes her learning. This is where you come in, because you observe your child in many different kinds of environments. Where is he most alert? Where does she access most of her abilities?

For instance, you now know that for many children sitting still is the worst thing for their learning, they need to be up and moving—movement may in fact help their brains process information. Often, for example, a child walking around, looking at the ceiling is very engaged, thinking deeply. If that is the case with your child, you need to communicate that to the classroom teacher who may not have this information and therefore may still think that children must sit down and look at the board to pay attention. You know your child's movement isn't something you want to stop; it is a sign of encouragement that information is being processed, as when a computer hums. Or if your daughter gets overwhelmed when she has to do long written assignments, you know this isn't because she is lazy, but rather because her mind needs extra time to output visual information.

You can teach your child's teacher about his or her mind, but you need first to become aware of what the most effective way to do that would be. Some teachers may feel threatened when they are offered this information. But it can be done. As playwright Edwin Freidman said, "People hear you when they are moving toward you, never when they are being pursued."

On the Same Side: Establishing a Dialogue

Problems don't exist *in* people but *between* them. It follows then that solutions we are searching for about how best to educate our children don't exist in the teacher, or the student, or the parent, but between them. I'd like to share an image and a process with you that I think provides a very powerful possible approach to finding those solutions.

This approach was inspired by a quantum physicist named David Bohm, who is developing a method and theory of dialogue. As he uses the term, dialogue is not the same as a back and forth discussion or argument. It is a process that happens between people when they are willing to suspend certainty together. The image he gives is of a stream flowing between two banks.

.I think of it this way: You the parent are sitting on one side of the stream, the teacher is sitting on the other side. Your child is sitting on a small bridge over the water. The stream is the dialogue that's between you, flowing in the same direction, even though you have different perspectives. Your thoughts and opinions are like leaves which float down the stream. Occasionally you find it possible to look into the reflection and see each other's perspective.

This is obviously different from an argument. There, your thoughts are like stones that first one of you throws into the stream and then the other, each trying to make his or her own point. Eventually these points build up into a dam which stops the flow of communication altogether.

What makes a dialogue work is that the people involved are willing to allow their ideas to float for a while. Not neccesarily to agree with each other, but to set your ideas down gently on the surface of the water and notice how they move between you. If there are differences, it helps to think that it is the ideas and how you hold on to them which are in conflict, not the people. This leads you to notice your ideas are producing consequences you don't want, and to ask yourself and each other, "What is my intention? What do we want to make happen now?"

It is also necessary to think of the person on the other bank, in this case, the teacher, as a friend or a colleague. Then you can be two allies with different opinions, instead of enemies or adversaries.

Obviously, you can't *make* the teacher or your child dialogue. Unless they've read this book or heard of Bohm's ideas, they won't even know what you're talking about. But *you* can be guided by the image. You can state your ideas specifically and explicitly. You can both advocate for your child and inquire into what the teacher's needs are. "Mr. Pomposity, what can the three of us do so that Jerome is excited about learning?" "Mrs. Chalkdust, there are some things I know about how Lonnie learns best that might help your time with her be a whole lot more effective and simple. What would be the best way for me to share that information with you? And what could I do at home to support what you are doing here?"

If you reach an impasse you can say what is making it difficult for you. You can say you want help finding ways that will work for all of you to overcome the barriers. You can ask what the teacher would need to change his or her mind.

I just sighed. I know I'm asking a lot of you. I wish we were all more skilled at creating dialogue. I wish we all grew up with parents and teachers and television stars and politicians who had modeled dialogue and effective communication. But we didn't. And just because we don't know how to do it, doesn't mean we can't think about it. Everything that exists in the world that humans have made—bridges and telephones, sculptures and symphonies, inoculations and the Bill of Rights—was created by someone who was frustrated with the status quo. Think about these ideas and use them like training wheels on a two-wheeler as you practice going down a bumpy road that few have traveled before.

Influence: A Butterfly's Approach

When people talk about children or education these days, they eventually get around to talking about control: who is out of it, who is in it, who has lost it. Classroom teachers and parents struggle for years trying to find it. Children struggle for years trying to avoid it.

Peter Senge, the director of MIT's Center for Organizational Learning, has this to say about control: "Helplessness, the belief that we cannot influence the circumstances under which we live, undermines the incentive to learn, as does the belief that someone somewhere else dictates our actions. Conversely, if we know our fate is in our own hands, our learning matters."

When parents, teachers, and children struggle with each other, it is often because they feel helpless in their ability to *influence* what is happening, and so they resort to *control*. What's the difference between the two? To answer that question, I'd like to offer you an experience which may help put your fate back in your own hands.

I learned this powerful little practice from Sensei Lloyd Miyashiro, a teacher of both a martial art form called Ki Aikido and high school students in Kauai, Hawaii:

Have someone extend one arm and make a fist. If there's no one around, do it with one of your own arms. First try to control *it by trying to move the fist.*

You will probably notice in a very short time that the more force you use, the more resistance or rebellion there will be on the part of the fist.

Now, try another way: influence. Place your thumb and index finger (of your other hand if you are doing this by yourself) on either side of the extended wrist as lightly as a butterfly. The lighter, the better. Don't try to do anything, just breathe and notice where movement already exists. Unless you are working with a corpse, there will be some very slight movement.

Notice how you can move with that fist for a while and then extend the direction of the movement whichever way it is naturally going. Lightly.

After a few minutes, it will probably be obvious to you that you can influence the direction of the movement, especially if you don't push. As soon as you get controlling, there will be resistance or rebellion. The more aware you are, the more possibilities there are for influence. It feels like a dance, and almost everyone would rather be danced with than pushed around.

I could do this practice a thousand times and still learn something new from it each time. You might imagine, as you are doing it, that the butterfly is you and the fist is your child's teacher. While you are doing it, you can allow yourself just to wonder, "What if this is how I was relating to her? I wonder how I'd be talking? What would my tone of voice be? What would I be doing? What is the best way to tell her what I know?" You won't need to "get answers." They will just emerge, pop into your mind.

Here's another possibility: what if you behaved toward your own mind, when it got stuck or stubborn, when it was confused or frustrated, the way you were with the fist?

While we're at it, you might want to imagine that the fist is your child. Wonder your way through some struggle you are having now by trying to control him or her. For example, "If this is Simon when he refuses to do his homework, and this is me, I wonder how I could influence him? What could I show him? How could I encourage him?"

Did you notice that when the fist was been pushed around, your attention shifted to wanting to fight against the hand pushing it? In a like manner, when there is coercion, children tend to shift focus from taking responsibility for their own behavior to fighting against "the boss." They have many weapons—acting out, dropping out, drugs, depression, suicide, pregnancy. Like the fist, they resist: "You can't make me!"

Teachers and parents cannot communicate effectively with each other when they are attempting to control the way the other person thinks, or coerce them into agreeing with their point of view. They cannot serve as mentors, enhance learning, or encourage children to become more responsible when they resort to control or coercion. A sword striking a sword produces a clash. But what happens if the sword strikes and it hits water?

We always have a choice as to how we respond to a child. Instead of bossing, we can help children overcome obstacles that stand in the way of their doing quality work in the classroom. If there is a problem with behavior, the child has to be guided to take responsibility for solving the problem. The adult insists there is a solution. "What were you doing when this problem started? Was it against the rules? How can we work it out so it doesn't happen again? What can I do to help you? What will you do? What if you don't? What consequence do you choose?"

All children in a classroom should be involved in making the rules and agreeing to them and to the consequences. Everyone should sign those rules. The teacher or parent doesn't need to punish, just to make sure the consequences are carried out. Parents and teachers need rules as well, such as "No sarcasm, no putting kids down, no humiliation or criticism of who they are. Listen to what they have to say."

I reflect now, years later, on some nasty confrontations I had with my son, various students, and some of their parents. I realize that, when the dust settled, when my rage had burned itself out and my tears had evaporated, I found myself not liking or respecting how *I* had been parenting or teaching even more than I didn't like what the other had been doing. If you had asked me in the moment, I probably wouldn't have admitted it, but that was the real truth.

To some of you this all can seem like Martian, since it may not be how your parents or teachers treated each other or you. Most people feel awkward when they first begin to practice influence instead of control. But awkward is part of learning something new, isn't it? Remember your first kiss? I wonder how you can make mistakes while learning something new without making yourself wrong.

The human race is supposed to evolve, to become more effective, more humane, more compassionate. Our culture is riddled with the sickness of violence and abuse. If we always do what we always did, we'll always get what we always got. Between an impulse and an act, we always have a choice as to how we respond. I wish my parents and my teachers had been more willing to choose to be awkward butterflies than lethal swordsmen. Let's hope our children don't end up wishing the same thing about us.

Living the Possible

Anne had a glorious experience recently of the kind of mentoring alliance that can be possible between parents and teachers: "As we sat around the oblong wooden table, the scene before me nearly filled my eyes with tears. This could have been a typical evaluation meeting, when the parents of a child who's struggling in school come to listen to the experts tell them what's wrong with their child. This could have been a tense hour, with a litany of test scores, and long faces and mother and father and teacher not knowing whether to feel guilty or to blame. Fortunately, that was not what happened at all.

"I had been consulting for the day with the teachers of Brimfield Elementary School: observing in classrooms, meeting with teachers, helping them to sort out the thinking patterns of the students they were curious about, brainstorming enjoyable, multi-perceptual ways to teach their curriculum. The kindergarten teacher asked me to sit in on this evaluation meeting after school. I was delighted. Allen, the five-year-old student, had also been one of the children I had observed that day.

"As his parents arrived, I realized Allen's mother had participated in the workshop I had given several months ago. I remembered her enthusiasm as she determined the patterns of her children. The other participants in the meeting were the school psychologist, the reading specialist, and the kindergarten teacher, all of whom were part of the training group in perceptual processing.

"John Castronova, the psychologist, a gentle, soft spoken man whose mind used the KVA pattern, began by briefly referring to his test results, almost as if getting the formalities out of the way. He leaned forward, folding his hands in front of him, and said, 'Now, the tests just confirm what we've been thinking—that Allen's mind uses the AKV pattern. What this means, as you know, is that he learns quite easily from what he hears and says, a strength we can use to support his creative, less accessible visual channel. It also helps us understand his blurting out things in the classroom and his difficulty recognizing numbers and letters. Let's talk for a few minutes about what's been working at home and in the classroom to support him in learning his basic skills.'"

"For forty-five minutes, we brainstormed what Allen needed and how we could help him and each other in ways that made him feel good about himself and followed the natural path of his learning.

"I felt as if I were part of a sacred circle of people with Allen in the middle, being held by the adults entrusted with his care, parents and teachers together. I knew I was witnessing the promise, the possibility that this way of thinking provides in the hands of loving adults who are eager to find a better way to understand and educate their children."

Creating a Possible Future

It doesn't take much time or cost very much money to teach people about perceptual processing. A day initially for adults, less time for children since they learn faster. Something magical happens when parents and teachers, administrators and specialists can all learn this together. It makes it obvious that everyone is on the same side with the same goals.

After that, what is needed is a few follow-up days, such as the one Anne described above, after people have had a chance to work with the ideas in their own lives, and lots of opportunities for practice and application. As in learning to ride a bicycle or holding yourself back when your child does, practice is the most important part. At first you'll have more questions than answers, feel awkward and unbalanced. But in a relatively short period of time, you'll ride along and have no more trouble than you do distinguishing a rosebush from a maple tree. What you're really learning is to become deeply curious about a natural process, the way thoughts move through different minds. And of course, to appreciate those differences as blessings.

There are more and more people imploring the powers that be in education to change the way they are thinking about children's talents and abilities. Howard Gardner, of Harvard University, suggests there are seven intelligences—linguistic, spatial, kinesthetic, musical, interpersonal, logical mathematical, intrapersonal. Calvin Taylor, at the University of Utah, talks about eight different talents we should be developing: productive or creative thought, planning, implementing a plan, decision making, forecasting, communications, human relations, and discerning opportunities. Robert Sternberg at Yale describes the Triarchic Mind, three kinds of intelligence: componential, contextual, and experiential.

These approaches are slightly different, one from the other, but in essence they are summed up by Carbo and Dunn: "Because of the extensive research that has been done [at St. John's University], and our own experience, we believe that children who have been taught through their natural learning styles *become* the achievers in school; those who experience difficulty do so because they are not being taught in ways that respond to how they learn. Thus we believe in identifying each student's unique characteristics and providing complementary methods and resources to insure academic success; there is nothing as important as determining each youngster's unique learning style."

In Zen Buddhism they say that a finger pointing to the moon should not be confused with the moon. This book is just one finger. It does not, cannot, contain all the "solutions" to all the problems we are facing in education today. To be honest, I'm not interested in education. I'm interested in children and learning. And what works and what doesn't.

I saw a bumper sticker recently that said: "If all else fails, lower your goals." I disagree. We've been trying that in education for years. In order to create possible futures, we have to change not just *what* we think, but our predominant ways of thinking about how our children learn.

In thinking of our challenge as mentors, a tale comes to mind. It is about an old man named Zusya who spent the last ten years of his life trying to be generous, kind, loving, perfect. As he aged, he got more and more depressed, because he was so fallible. Finally, his wife called in the village wise man. He came and sat at Zusya's side and listened deeply to him. "I've tried my best to be like Moses, but I am a wretched failure at it."

The wise man was quiet for a long time. Then he said in a very insistent voice, "But my friend, you have not failed. When you die, God will not ask you why you weren't more like Moses. You will only be asked why you weren't more like Zusya!"

Our children are being pressured to be unique in the same way as everybody else. It is our responsibility to discover and honor their individual uniqueness, to support their forming minds taking the shape that is truly their own.

When considering the massive changes that are needed in our schools, most experts would agree with Howard Gardner: "I believe that we will not be able to improve our educational system materially in the next decade; fulfilling that assignment will take several decades. All that we can determine by the year 2000 is whether we are serious about bringing about major changes."

Most experts say we care less, vote less, know less, these days. I am not an expert. I am a parent and a teacher. I think of your children and mine, Brian and David, Jerome and Jordan, Raoul, Isabella, and Gregor. I imagine telling them that their wounded minds will have to wait several decades. That people don't care enough, know enough, vote enough. I write those words and it is as if the writing were making an incision, as if those children's minds and all they are capable of being were cut open.

What can *you* do about all of this? Live out these questions for the next few months: How can you connect with school administrators and teachers in a way that honors their expertise, while expanding their awareness about individual learning differences? How can you make a difference for the kids that have been taught they are dumb, disabled, garbage because words come slowly to them, or they are creatively coordinated, or they jiggle when they have to sit too long? What do you know now that could help one of them find a jewel in that garbage? Is there a child in you that yearns to be taught how he or she is smart? Is there an eagle in your house that has been haphazardly disguised as a chicken? How *can* you make a difference?

Our children are our future selves. They are the ones who must be given power, resources, and skills to create possible futures. We can support each other. We can use each other to revitalize our vision, to rekindle the flame, to salve the wounds and save the minds of our children. You do have influence. You can make choices. You are important. The only mistake you can make is thinking one person can't make a difference.

Appendix:

A Teaching Primer

*"Students can no longer learn in isolation
sitting by themselves at their desks, but
by working together to reach solutions
and answers in a cooperative fashion. If
you accept this concept, you immediately
reject the traditional idea of a teacher
standing up in front of a classroom and
lecturing or reading out of a textbook."*
—Gary Watts, Senior Director,
Center for Innovation,
National Education Association

This appendix expands on the information in Chapters 5-10, offering guidelines for meeting the specific educational needs of each pattern, as well as how particular subject matter can be taught to meet those needs. It is designed to be used by teachers, tutors, and homeschooling parents, as well as by parents who wish to share such information with their child's classroom teacher. Please bear in mind that these are just suggestions— each teacher also has unique ways of presenting material.

Teaching AKV Children

In general, AKVs learn best by hearing and discussing or repeating what they have heard. They need to have time to put what they are learning into their own words. They can be good teachers for other children; this will reinforce their learning, allow them to talk and to feel useful. Working with other children of the same pattern will give them the chance to speak what they know at a pace that suits them and get practice listening to others. Moving while they listen will involve more of their minds and help them absorb what they hear.

AKV children demand a lot of verbal attention. It's important that there be time in class for their questions. They tend to be mumblers while they are working. They need space in the classroom where they can talk quietly to themselves while studying or taking tests without disturbing others. AKVs can easily memorize what they have heard, particularly if it has rhythm to it. Making up rhymes or cheers will help, especially with spelling words or vocabulary. The learning will go deeper than rote memory if they can find a way to relate new concepts to their personal experience. They will remember the word "alternatives," for example, when they can think of some that they have in their lives.

AKV children work quite well with background noise. In fact, some of them may need to be hearing something, such as the radio playing, in order to study well, especially if they are reading; perhaps they could bring a Walkman to use in the classroom if they need it.

It is likely that reading and writing assignments will be challenging for these students. They need to be taught to read with a whole language approach, where they write stories from their experience and then learn to read the words they have written as whole words in context. They need freedom to choose books of high interest to them. They may be very likely to select books with large print, blank space on most pages, and lots of pictures.

Learning to form letters may be laborious. It might be helpful for them to write big, especially at first, so their eyes don't have to focus on tiny print. They may need to learn letters, numbers, and sight words in some associative way: writing the letter A might be "Up the mountain, down the mountain, across the bridge in a car."

Learning to type or use a word processor may really help older AKVs find more ease in writing. They may always need more time to finish written work than others. If possible, verbal options or shortened reading and writing assignments should be offered, since they easily space out with too much detailed written information. They may need to read written directions out loud or to tell someone what they've understood in their own words.

What AKVs write or draw and what they receive in writing is very special to them. It is preferable to talk to them about their assignments, or write notes on another sheet, rather than visually mark up their papers. It may mean a lot to them to receive notes of encouragement or congratulations.

There need to be places in the classroom which are visually spacious, not filled up with things to see and read, where AKVs might rest their eyes. Sitting near the windows may allow these kids the larger visual perspective they need so they can focus more easily when they are required to. Teachers should remember that these children will be eye shy--they usually listen without making eye contact.

AKVs' organizational style is not based on visual neatness. They tend to be pilemakers. They may need help in discovering their way to keep track of things. These kids are great idea people. They need support to talk out, think through, evaluate, and manifest their creative ideas. They can also really shine with creative problem-solving skills.

AKV children have a lot of physical energy. Allowing them freedom to move and opportunities to be physically active will help keep them alert in class. For this reason, a learning centers approach seems to work well for them. They also need to actually try different options in order to decide what works best. Frequent choices in activities is important in their learning process.

Teaching AVK Children

AVK children learn most easily from listening and discussing. It is helpful to them to have a verbal outline of what is going to be covered in a lesson, activity, or lecture. This could be as simple as saying, "Today we are going to talk about the causes of the Civil War." This gives their minds an organizing framework into which they can put the information that follows.

Provide opportunities for AVKs to talk. They need to put what they are learning into their own words out loud so they can hear what they are thinking. This need can be used well in the classroom. Ask them to summarize a concept or a lesson for the entire class. Find ways for them to teach others when possible. Create a group of similar pattern study buddies who can discuss what they've read or learned together at their typical fast, conceptual pace. Set aside time often when they can ask their almost endless supply of questions.

The phonetic approach to learning to read works well with AVK students. They tend to subvocalize or read out loud softly to themselves, especially when first learning. Provide space in the classroom where this can happen without disturbing others. AVKs tend to be avid readers; many of them love to devour factual information.

Support their curiosity and motivation to learn. Allow them to work at their own pace on projects of their choosing. Invite them to share with the class what they are learning. Encourage them to stretch beyond "right" answers into the realms of unanswerable questions and researched opinions. Teach them in age-appropriate ways how to thoroughly investigate what they are most curious about.

Provide them with a broad range of writing skills. Guide them step-by-step verbally through paper organization. Use visual aids or visualizations to help awaken the imaginative levels of their minds. Invite them to write poetry or to make up their own language. Help them find ways to use their intellect to go deeper.

Hands-on projects or experiments may be quite challenging for AVK learners. Allow them enough space and time not to feel pressured. Explain and demonstrate physical activities in small steps, using metaphors where possible. For example, in an electricity experiment you might say, "Now wrap the wire around the tube like you're winding a string on a yo-yo." Allow them to ask as many questions as they need to before trying.

Teaching KAV Children

Providing hands-on, concrete experiences is the most effective way to teach KAV children. They will learn best what they find immediately useful or related in some way to their past experience. Whenever possible, they should act things out, create physical representations, or make models of what they are learning. They can most easily remember what they've done themselves, particularly if it involves touching, smelling, or tasting. In studying the eye, for example, instead of reading or looking at diagrams, it would help these kids to have a model they could take apart and talk about.

KAVs learn best when they actually embody what they are learning. If they are studying place value in math, invite them to get up and become the number in the hundredths place. Then, follow this by pointing out which places are used to write money.

KAVs need frequent movement breaks and the freedom to

move while listening. It is often helpful to have objects and clay available that they can hold or manipulate to keep themselves alert.

They work well in groups, with companionship or frequent side-by-side check-ins from the teacher. They respond well, quite literally, to a pat on the back.

Reading and writing tend to be difficult to learn and do in any quick manner for KAVs. They need to be taught to read with a whole language approach, where they write stories from their experience and then learn to read the words they have written as whole words in context. Relevance is especially important here; these kids need to choose books that they really want to read. They may consistently choose activity-oriented topics and "easy" books with lots of space and pictures. They may have more success reading while in motion than sitting still. Using a rocking chair or riding a stationary bike might help.

Reading instructions is often difficult for KAV children, who will do better with oral directions, or when allowed to figure something out with their hands and by doing first.

First writing experiences should be dictations directly from their lives. When possible, allow them more time to complete written work, make reading and writing assignments more brief, or provide alternatives to such assignments. KAVs will have more success demonstrating their learning in projects, discussions, or skits than in written tests or reports. When they must write, suggest they walk and dictate what they want to say into a tape recorder which they can later transcribe.

Handwriting and spelling can be tedious for these children. It is helpful for them to use their bodies and their voices as much as possible in these subjects. Have them learn their letters by writing them very large, perhaps standing at the chalkboard or easel so they can use their whole body in the process. Practice spelling by tracing letters in the air, in sand, fingerpaint, or shaving cream while reciting out loud.

What KAVs write or draw, and what they receive in writing, has a profound effect on them. Talk to them about their assignments, or write notes on another sheet, rather than visually mark up their papers. It may mean a lot to them to receive notes of encouragement or congratulations.

Keep in mind that KAVs space out with too much detailed written information. Make sure there are places in the classroom which are visually spacious, not filled up with things to see and read, and point out that KAVs might enjoy resting their eyes there. Allow them to sit near the windows so that, within limits, their eyes may choose bigger vistas to look at. This will help when they are required to focus. Remember that these children will be eye shy—it's best not to require them to look at you. Know that they can listen without making sustained eye contact.

Do not expect KAVs to be visually organized. They tend to be pilemakers. Help them discover an organizational style that works for them. Encourage them to use a lot of space on written work.

Teaching KVA Children

KVA children absorb information most easily when provided with hands-on learning opportunities. They learn well on field trips, with models, or real-life objects, when they can actually smell, touch, feel, and see what is being referred to in words. Make learning experiences as concrete and relevant as possible. If they are learning about money and how to make change, for example, they need to practice with actual cash and coins, over and over again. They can then see the results of their actions, and make their own corrections, if needed.

Find out what KVAs want to know about the subject matter

so that they will feel both their own involvement in the learning process and its relevance in their lives.

Provide experiences where they do things first before they are explained or shown. If you are studying the properties of float and sink in science, for example, let them experiment on their own, testing various objects, even before you demonstrate or explain what you are learning. If you must show them what to do, allow them to do what they've seen and then ask questions about it. Words in the middle of a demonstration can cause confusion. If you must explain, teach tasks in small steps and give them a model or diagram to follow as well as oral directions.

Teach and review things in an active, game-like way, where KVAs can be up and moving, visually alert and challenged but not required to speak long sentences on their own.

With these children, it is especially important to provide ways to learn and express what they've learned that involve more than simply listening and speaking. Listening comprehension may be next to impossible all by itself. Encourage KVAs to take notes, to use flashcards, to draw, doodle, or play with clay when they are listening or studying. In reading, use books and tapes together. Invite these children to look at the pictures and use their fingers to keep their place. Have them try rocking, moving, or standing while they read. This may increase their ability to concentrate.

Find alternatives for oral presentations. Encourage them to demonstrate learning with projects or plays that engage their hands and bodies. Allow them to use props and visuals, and to prepare ahead of time when they must present orally.

Avoid putting these kids on the spot to speak. They get more anxious than most with round-robin exercises. Provide opportunities where they can take the time they need to consider a question. Movement can often help them find their words.

Encourage them to take a walk or pace when they are thinking about something, even while taking a test or writing a paper. Use touch as a way to calm the school anxiety of typical KVAs. Let them know with a pat on the back that you are with them as they learn.

Find creative ways to help these kids expand their speaking vocabulary. They often feel like they don't know what they know, and they don't have the words to express what they feel. Be aware of the need for moments of silence in the learning process. These children can easily space out with too many words. Teach KVAs to know when they have had enough verbal input and encourage them to request pauses. Perhaps develop a classroom signal, a bell, a light, or a sign, for just this purpose. Provide a silent area in the room where they can concentrate and not have to sort out the distracting sounds around them.

Teaching VKA Children

VKA children will be helped most in the classroom with the use of visual aids and opportunities to move and experience what they are learning. Provide written as well as oral instructions for these children. If lecturing, give them an outline to follow. Encourage them to take notes or make mind maps (clusters of symbols or pertinent words which can record information in a non-linear form). Break up lengthy lectures with experiential exercises and, where possible, include demonstrations, charts, diagrams, pictures, or other visual materials.

Use a sight decoding method for teaching VKAs to read. They do well with flashcards. You can support their comprehension by encouraging VKAs to use their natural ability to visualize to make pictures in their minds of what they are reading.

Skills of all kinds can be most easily grasped by showing

VKAs how to do something and then letting them try it, if possible without words at first. Allow them to do what they've seen and then ask questions about it. Words in the middle of a demonstration can cause confusion. Teach things in small steps.

Nurture feelings of competence in these kids. Offer several options of how to do something and allow them to choose. Encourage them to try something and then notice how they feel. Allow them to change options in the middle. The important thing is to give them chances to discover what alternatives are the most satisfying.

Finding relevance in new information can be a key to effective learning for VKAs. Invite them to discover how whatever they're learning reminds them of what they've already learned or is related to what they've experienced in the past. This will aid the retention of new material.

Find easy, non-threatening ways for VKAs to get familiar with the sensations in their bodies. Physical activity can help them become aware of how they feel. Encourage them to pursue some form of exercise or develop a hobby that uses their hands. Help them find the most comfortable study places and positions, and to learn individually what works best.

Provide alternatives for oral reports, when possible. If VKAs must practice speaking in front of others, encourage them to use notes, to move as they speak, and to select topics related to their own experience.

Avoid putting these kids on the spot to speak. Provide opportunities where they can take the time they need to consider a question. Movement can often help them find their words. Writing can help them find clarity of thought. Encourage them to take a walk or pace when they are thinking about something, even while taking a test or writing a paper.

Find creative ways to help VKAs expand their speaking vocabulary so they will have the words they need to express what they know and feel. Encourage them to write creatively, to express as often as possible the feelings they have inside.

VKAs need moments of silence so their brains can assimilate verbal input instead of spacing out with too many words. They can be taught to know when they have had enough so that they can request pauses in all the speaking. A bell, light, or sign can be used for just this purpose. Provide a silent area in the room where these children can concentrate and not have to sort out the distracting sounds around them.

Teaching VAK Children

Most subjects, as typically taught, come quite easily to VAK learners. They learn easily from what they read and are shown. The phonetic approach works well for them in learning to read. They can be clear, concise writers and good proofreaders. Encourage them to explore a wide range of writing styles including personal stories, dialogue, poetry, and imaginative prose.

VAK students generally like to take notes, although they may rarely go back to them. Merely writing things fills the need to see what is being said. Handouts work well for them. They can cope quite well with written instructions alone, although a verbal check-in may insure their understanding. They also respond well to typical testing. They tend to prefer cramming for a test. New information doesn't always stay with them unless they have used more than their visual channel to learn and integrate it. Alternative options, such as projects, plays, and oral reports take these children into their stretch learning zone and should be encouraged.

VAKs can work fairly independently on most school work, especially reading and writing assignments. Allowing them to coach and teach other students helps to reinforce what they have learned. Pattern study groups would also work well for VAKs.

They need time to discuss and sort their opinions out loud.

In the more experiential subjects, especially science, upper level math, physical education, and vo-tech subjects, VAKs need to be shown and talked through new skills before trying a task themselves. In studying the parts of a flower, for example, they would do well working with a study partner, looking at a well-labeled, colorful diagram, and discussing the functions of each part. Ideally, a teacher or partner could talk them through each stage of the dissection process.

It may be difficult for VAK kids to learn structured physical activities. They may need a lot of specific, patient attention when learning to use their hands or bodies. When learning physical skills, they first need to be shown what they are going to do and told why it is an important thing to know, particularly how it fits in to a larger set of skills or learnings. Then they need to be given a metaphor for each step in the process, a visual image that will represent what their body will look like while doing it. For example, you might say, "Pretend your body is a clock. To begin this warm-up exercise, your arms are like the hands at 2 and 10."

Next, VAKs need to be talked through the skill one small, slow step at a time using the same metaphor: "Now move your arms so they are at 3 and 9 on your clock." At this phase, they also need verbal feedback about what they are doing right. Finally, they need to practice on their own, as privately as possible, so they can build confidence. Allow these students to take their time and to learn one step at a time.

Although VAK learners are successful in school for the most part, they can come away having made good grades but feeling like they haven't learned much. As often as possible, offer opportunities which help new information come alive and go in deeper. Don't just read about animals, go pet them. Don't just look at pottery, make it. Don't just study a play, perform it.

Suggestions For Teaching Different Subjects

Reading: A phonics approach is needed initially for VAKs and AVKs; decoding and sight method for VKAs; whole language and experiential methods for KAVs, KVAs, and AKVs. For all patterns, comprehension needs to be stressed over rote drills.

Writing: Early writing should emphasize meaning over spelling and grammar. KAVs and AKVs will have difficulty with long reading and writing assignments, especially under time pressure. Since they absorb written material more slowly and more deeply, they should be given more time or briefer assignments. Written exams are also difficult for them. It is more effective to have them write from their own experience or tape reports on what they read and then transcribe the tape. VKAs and KVAs may have difficulty with oral presentations unless they have written down what they plan to say. AVKs and VAKs should shine here if they are interested in what they are reading and writing.

Mathematics: A hands-on approach will work best for VKAs and KVAs, showing rather than telling; words will get in the way. AKVs and AVKs need to see the whole of mathematical models and discuss them. KAVs need to have concrete experiences which they can talk about. VAKs do well when working in teams and teaching concepts to other children.
Science: KVAs, VKAs, and KAVs learn best by experimenting first and then discussing in small groups. AKVs, AVKs, and VAKs need to discuss before and during experimentation.

History and Social Studies: AVKs will do especially well here. KAVs and AKVs should be given options to demonstrate what they know besides long written reports and tests, such as making oral presentations, plays, etc., and be given other ways to assimilate the information besides long reading assignments.

VKAs and KVAs should be encouraged to make costumes, maps, models, etc. AVKs and VAKs should write stories and make tapes of written material.

Foreign Languages: VKAs and KVAs may develop a good accent but have difficulty with spoken vocabulary unless they have direct experiences. KAVs and AKVs may have difficulty if they learn to read the language before or instead of speaking it. AVKs and VAKs do better to read it and speak it simultaneously. The ability to communicate should be first priority. Classes need to emphasize using the language they are learning in an everyday way, ie., learning the top ten most popular songs, writing letters, etc.

Music: Reading music may be difficult for KAVs and AKVs who may love to sing and play instruments. AVKs may have difficulty singing and playing rhythm instruments at the same time. KVAs and VKAs can learn to harmonize and hear the whole of music, as well as compose. VAKs can do wonderful percussion and write lyrics with ease.

Visual Arts: This can be very effective for helping VKAs and KVAs express feelings they cannot speak. AVKs and VAKs may need to talk while they work. AKVs and KAVs do better with 3-D media and may be very shy, yet profoundly creative about what they produce. In general, visual arts should be taught so students can learn to express themselves and at the same time solve problems and develop critical thinking skills.

Physical Education and Vo-Tech: KAVs, VKAs, and KVAs should be able to just get out and do, or watch and do. VAKs and AVKs will need verbal instructions that are slow and metaphoric before they can do anything. They may have trouble doing repeated, structured exercises. AKVs need to describe what they are going to do first, and they make wonderful coaches for other students.

Bibliography

Armstrong, Thomas, Ph.D. *Awakening Your Child's Natural Genius: Enhancing Curiosity, Creativity, and Learning Ability.* Los Angeles: J.P. Tarcher, 1991.

Burns, Marilyn. *I Am Not A Short Adult.* Boston: Little, Brown & Co., 1977.

____. *The I Hate Mathematics Book.* Boston: Little, Brown & Co., 1975.

Carbo, Marie, Rita Dunn and Kenneth Dunn. *Teaching Students to Read Through Their Individual Learning Styles.* Englewood Cliffs, NJ: Prentice Hall, 1986.

Dunn, Rita and Kenneth Dunn. *Bringing Out the Giftedness in Your Child: Nurturing Every Child's Unique Strengths, Talents and Potential.* New York: John Wiley & Sons, 1992.

Faber, Adele, and Elaine Mazlish. *How to Talk So Kids Will Listen and Listen So Kids Will Talk.* New York: Avon Books, 1982.

Gardner, Howard. *The Unschooled Mind.* New York: Harper Collins, 1991.

Gatto, John Taylor. *Dumbing Us Down: The Hidden Curriculum of Compulsory Schooling.* Philadelphia, Pa.: New Society Publishers, 1992.

Glasser, William, M.D. *The Quality School.* New York: Harper Perennial, 1990.

Haley, Jay. *Uncommon Therapy: The Psychiatric Techniques of Milton H. Erickson, MD.* New York: Norton, 1973.

Hall, Edward T. *Beyond Culture.* Garden City, NY: Anchor Press/Doubleday & Co., 1976.

Herbert, Cindy and Susan Russell. *Everychild's Everyday: Learning About Learning.* Garden City, NY: Anchor Press/Doubleday & Co., Inc., 1980.

Kimmel, Margaret Mary and Elizabeth Segel. *For Reading Out Loud!: A Guide to Sharing Books With Children.* New York: Delacorte Press, 1983.

Liedloff, Jean. *The Continuum Concept.* New York: Alfred A. Knopf, 1977.

Markova, Dawna. *The Art of the Possible: A Compassionate Approach to Understanding the Way People Think, Learn and Communicate.* Berkeley, Ca: Conari Press, 1990.

New Games Foundation, Andrew Fluegelman, Ed. *The New Games Book.* Garden City, NY: Dolphin/Doubleday & Co., 1976.

Ostrander, Sheila, Lynn Schroeder, with Nancy Ostrander. *Superlearning.* New York: Dell Publishing Company, 1979.

Pearce, Joseph Chilton. *Magical Child.* New York: E.P. Dutton, 1977.

____. *Magical Child Matures.* New York: E.P. Dutton, 1981.

Perry, Susan K. *Playing Smart: A Parent's Guide to Enriching, Offbeat Learning Activities for Ages 4-14.* Minneapolis, MN: Free Spirit Publishing Inc., 1990.

Samples, Bob. *Openmind/Wholemind: Parenting and Teaching Tomorrow's Children Today.* Rolling Hills Estates, CA: Jalmar Press, 1987.

Samples, Bob, Cheryl Samples and Dick Barnhart. *The Wholeschool Book.* Reading, Ma: Addison-Wesley, 1977.

Senge, Peter. *The Fifth Discipline: The Art and Practice of the Learning Organization.* New York: Doubleday/Currency, 1990.

Stevenson, Harold W. and James W. Stigler. *The Learning Gap: Why Our Schools Are Failing and What We Can Learn From Japanese and Chinese Education.* New York: Summit, 1992.

Further Resources

If you want to know more about personal thinking patterns, you might like to read *THE ART OF THE POSSIBLE: A COMPASSIONATE APPROACH TO UNDERSTANDING THE WAY PEOPLE THINK, LEARN AND COMMUNICATE* ($12.95) by Dawna Markova, Ph.D.

Companion audio tapes of HOW YOUR CHILD IS SMART ($9.95) and THE ART OF THE POSSIBLE ($9.95) are also available. Each is a 90-minute interview with Dawna Markova conducted by Jean Feraca of Wisconsin Public Radio.

To order the book or tapes, contact Conari Press at 1-800-685-9595.

◆ ◆ ◆

To obtain a list of consultants trained in this approach or to find out about seminars for parents given by Dr. Markova, contact Conari Press at the above number.

◆ ◆ ◆

Index